WHAT WAS
WATERGATE?

WHAT WAS
WATERGATE?

PAMELA KILIAN

A THOMAS DUNNE BOOK

St. Martin's Press
New York

Design by Maura Fadden Rosenthal

Library of Congress Cataloging-in-Publication Data

Kilian, Pamela.
    What was Watergate?
        p.   cm.
    "A Thomas Dunne book."
    Summary: Recounts the events of the political scandal
known as Watergate, which resulted in the resignation of
President Nixon.
    ISBN 0-312-04446-1
    1. Watergate Affair, 1972–1974—Juvenile literature.
2. Nixon, Richard M. (Richard Milhous), 1913–
—Juvenile literature.   [1. Watergate Affair,
1972–1974.   2. Nixon, Richard M. (Richard Milhous),
1913–   .]   I. Title.
E860.K55   1990   973.924—dc20   89-77806   CIP   AC

First Edition

10 9 8 7 6 5 4 3 2 1

CONTENTS

WHAT WAS
WATERGATE?

1

THE BREAK-IN

FRANK WILLS WAS A NIGHT WATCHMAN AT THE WATERGATE hotel-apartment-office complex in Washington, D.C., just a few blocks from the White House. Not long after he began work at midnight on Saturday, June 17, 1972, Wills found tape over a lock on a basement door of the Watergate, which would have allowed someone to enter the building without being detected. He thought maybe the building engineer had taped the door open while he worked, but in any case, Wills knew the tape should not be there. He removed it.

Later, during his 2:00 A.M. rounds, Wills checked the basement again. To his surprise, he found that the lock on the door had been retaped. It was clear that someone had been fooling around with the lock. Now Wills was taking no chances. He called the police.

Three officers arrived a few minutes later and began to search the building, floor by floor. They had their guns drawn but they were dressed in plainclothes. One could not tell just by their appearance that they were policemen. They found what they were looking for on the sixth floor.

Before the police arrived, something very curious had been happening on the sixth floor. Five men had been trying for half an hour to break into a suite of offices. They were not very efficient burglars.

Finally they got into the offices by taking the door off its hinges. Then two of the men stood guard outside the offices while the other three got to work inside.

These burglars were not working alone. Their accomplices were nearby. One of them was E. Howard Hunt, Jr., a former CIA agent, who was waiting in another part of the Watergate building, staying in touch with the "boss" of the operation, G. Gordon Liddy. Another was Alfred Baldwin, who was in a room at the Howard Johnson Motor Lodge, located directly across the street from the Watergate. His job was to watch the street to see who went into the Watergate. If the police, or anyone else who might endanger the burglary, arrived, he was to notify the burglars on a walkie-talkie.

From his room at the Howard Johnson, Baldwin also could see directly into the suite of offices where the burglars were working. He stood out on the balcony of his room to keep watch over everything.

Baldwin saw the three men drive up to the Watergate and go inside, but he did not recognize them as police officers because they were not in uniform. Also, they had long hair, which was fashionable at the time among young people but not generally with policemen. These three undercover cops looked more like hippies than policemen.

So Baldwin did not realize that anything was wrong until he suddenly saw the lights go on in the Watergate offices where the burglars were working—burglars generally do not turn on lights to advertise their presence. Baldwin felt panicky. But before he could do anything, two men walked out of one of the lighted Watergate offices and onto the balcony. Baldwin, standing directly across from them on his own balcony, was really worried now. He looked at the men and they looked at him. Since Baldwin did not actually know what the burglars looked like, he was not sure whether the men on the balcony were friend or foe.

He quickly ducked back into the hotel room, headed for his walkie-talkie, and called the burglars. But they could not hear him. Because the static coming from their walkie-talkie had been so loud—they feared it would be heard by others in the building—they had turned it off.

To Baldwin's relief, fellow accomplice Howard Hunt was standing by when the frantic call came.

"Are our people dressed casually or are they in suits?" Baldwin asked Hunt.

"Our people are in suits," Hunt replied.

Baldwin looked again at the men on the Watergate balcony. They were not wearing business suits. The burglars had to be in trouble.

When the police arrived at the sixth-floor suite, they entered through a back door and immediately turned on the lights. The burglars guarding the front door slipped inside the offices unseen to warn their colleagues, but there was no way they could get out without being detected.

While the officers searched other parts of the suite, all five of the men ducked behind a wooden screen around a desk in a still-dark cubicle and held their breath. They hoped the policemen would just look around briefly and not discover their hiding place.

But one of the policemen approached the cubicle where the men were hiding, saw a slight motion, and then spotted an arm.

"Hold it and come out," the officer said.

"Don't shoot, we give up," said the men.

The police were surprised when the lights went on. These were not your typical burglars. They were middle-aged men, in their forties and fifties, wearing business suits and thin rubber gloves, the kind used by surgeons. They carried cameras and film, a turned-off walkie-talkie, lock picks, and electronic surveillance equipment.

They had not actually stolen anything of value from the office. Instead, they were putting something in—little electronic "bugs" that would allow Baldwin in the Howard Johnson's across the street to hear what people in the Watergate offices said on the telephone.

This particular office belonged to a man named Larry O'Brien, chairman of the Democratic National Committee, whose job it was to aid political candidates in the Democratic party in getting elected. His main priority in 1972 was to help the Democratic candidate for president, Senator George McGovern. A lot of people were interested in O'Brien's private conversations.

The police did not know all of this when they made the arrests, though, and the burglars were not talking. At first they would not even give their real names. Each had a false identification.

The men spent the rest of the night at a police station. Later that morning two lawyers came to confer with them and advised them to tell the police their real names, which they did—James W. McCord, Jr., Bernard L. Barker, Frank A. Sturgis, Virgilio R. Gonzalez, and Eugenio R. Martinez. All except McCord lived in Miami. They had checked into the Watergate Hotel as guests on Friday.

By the time the five men were taken to court that afternoon, and formally charged with second-degree burglary, their case had caught the eye of editors at the local morning newspaper, the *Washington Post*. A young reporter, Bob Woodward, was assigned to cover the court hearing.

Woodward did not think the case sounded too interesting at first, but he perked up when one of the burglars, James McCord, was asked what he did for a living.

"Security consultant," McCord replied.

The judge asked where he worked. McCord said he had retired recently from the Central Intelligence Agency, or CIA.

This was surprising. The CIA is one of the most secretive agencies in the federal government. It tries to find out what other countries, or groups in other countries, are doing and make sure they do not harm the United States. Its agents are not supposed to spy on Americans.

Woodward thought it was strange that a former CIA agent would have taken part in a burglary at the Democratic party's headquarters. The Democrats are not foreigners; nor are they enemies of the country. Something odd had to be going on.

Woodward went back to his newspaper and wrote a story about the Watergate burglary. The editors put the story on the front page of the Sunday newspaper.

Other reporters and politicians were interested in the case too. They soon discovered that McCord not only was a former CIA agent, he now worked for the Committee for the Re-election of the President. This was a Republican group formed to help President Richard M. Nixon win a second term in office.

Larry O'Brien was head of the opposition party and had frequent telephone conversations with the men who were running for president on the Democratic side.

The election, on November 8, 1972, was only five months away. Had the president's men been spying on his opponents?

Absolutely not, said John N. Mitchell, the president's campaign manager and head of his reelection committee.

"We want to emphasize that this man and the other people involved were not operating either on our behalf or with our consent," Mitchell said when reporters asked him about the burglary. "There is no place in our campaign or in the electoral process for this type of activity, and we will not permit or condone it."

But just two weeks after the arrests, Mitchell resigned from the president's reelection committee.

Reporters at the White House also were curious about the case. They asked if anyone in the White House knew about either the burglary or the burglars. President Nixon's press secretary, Ronald L. Ziegler, whose job was to tell the reporters what was going on at the White House, said no one there knew anything about the Watergate break-in. "I am not going to comment from the White House on a third-rate alleged burglary attempt," he said.

Five days after the burglary, President Nixon himself denied that the White House had been involved. Two years later he would be forced to resign because of it.

What had happened?

2

HOW WATERGATE STARTED

THE BURGLARY AT THE WATERGATE WAS NOT AN ISOLATED event. It was just one of several troubling and illegal actions that took place during Richard Nixon's first term as president, secrets that were revealed years later.

At the time, the United States was deeply involved in the Vietnam War. To understand what happened during Watergate it is necessary to know something about the atmosphere in the country during that period.

Vietnam is a small country in Southeast Asia, thousands of miles from America. In the 1960s it was politically divided, with a Communist dictatorship controlling the northern half and a dictator friendly to Western countries holding power in the southern half. There also were Communist groups in South Vietnam who were trying to topple the government.

After John F. Kennedy was elected president in 1960, the United States began sending advisers to help the South Vietnamese plan their defense against the Communist guerrilla groups. When Kennedy was assassinated in November 1963, Lyndon B. Johnson became president. He sent more advisers and a lot of soldiers to help the South Vietnamese government.

By the mid-1960s many Americans had grown concerned about U.S. involvement in Vietnam. They felt that a large country like the United States should not get bogged down in the civil war of a small, distant country like Vietnam. And they did not understand why American soldiers should fight and die in Vietnam when the Communists there were no threat to us.

Other Americans felt differently. They said it was important to keep communism from spreading and to support democracies, no matter where in the world the fight occurred. They believed that the United States could keep the Communists from taking over South Vietnam.

Disagreements about Vietnam deeply divided the country. Massive street marches against the war took place on college campuses and in Washington, D.C. Many young men refused to go to Vietnam to fight.

The battle over the war was reflected in the presidential election as well. By 1968 President Johnson's policies on the war were so unpopular that he decided not to run for a second term in the White House. He thought he would be defeated.

That set off a scramble for the Democratic presidential nomination. One of the candidates, Robert Kennedy, was assassinated. A senator named Eugene McCarthy became the favorite of many people who opposed the war. Vice President Hubert Humphrey also was in the race.

When the Democrats gathered in Chicago in the summer of 1968 to choose their presidential candidate, there were bitter feelings on all sides. In addition, the streets of Chicago were filled with antiwar demonstrators, many of whom were beaten up by the police.

Humphrey won the Democratic nomination that year, but the ugly atmosphere at the convention and the divisions among the Democratic party members left him weakened. In the general election that November, Richard Nixon, the Republican presidential candidate, was the victor.

Nixon had promised during the election campaign that he had a plan to end the Vietnam War. Yet the war continued. More Americans were sent to fight. The number of street marches—demonstrations against the war—increased. Some people who initially had supported the war began turning against it.

Nixon was upset by the demonstrations and by people who opposed the war. He said he would try to end the fighting and bring "peace with honor" but that he did not want American forces to simply pull out of Vietnam. He wanted to defeat the Communists. And he wanted to punish the people who opposed or undermined his policies. He suspected that foreign countries unfriendly to the United States might be behind some of the demonstrations.

On May 9, 1969, the *New York Times* revealed that the United States had been secretly bombing Cambodia, a country bordering Vietnam. The bombings, which started in March 1969—just a couple of months after Nixon became president—were aimed at North Vietnamese troops hiding in Cambodia. But Cambodia was not officially involved in the war, so many people thought it was wrong for the United States to drop bombs there.

Because the White House knew there would be widespread opposition, the bombings had been kept secret from everyone except a few of Nixon's aides and several top men at the Pentagon, the U.S. military headquarters in Washington, D.C. Even Congress was not told about it.

The president was angry that the secret bombings had been publicly disclosed, even though he was required by law to tell Congress about such an act of war. He decided to try and find out who had informed the *New York Times* about the bombings.

Three days after the *Times* story appeared, an electronic "bug"—a wiretap—was put on the telephone of a government official suspected of secretly giving information about the bombing to the newspaper. This wiretap allowed the White House to listen to the man's private telephone conversations.

It was the first of seventeen wiretaps the Nixon administration installed in attempts to find out who was "leaking" information about the bombings and other foreign policy decisions that President Nixon was trying to keep secret. The conversations of four news reporters and thirteen government workers with important jobs were recorded over the next twenty-two months. Reports on the conversations were sent to the White House.

All of these wiretaps were secret. The White House never asked for permission to install them.

The law requires government officials to obtain a judge's permission for a wiretap, because no one's conversation should be secretly recorded unless there is a very good reason. One of the basic freedoms in the United States is the freedom of speech. If people are afraid that others are listening in on their conversations, they will not feel comfortable to speak freely. So installing wiretaps without a judge's permission undermines our right to freedom of speech.

As it turned out, the White House never did find out who told the *New York Times* about the secret bombings. All of the wiretaps had been a waste of time. President Nixon later claimed that he did not need a judge's permission for the wire-taps because what he was trying to find out was important to the nation's security. The U.S. Supreme Court rejected his ar-gument, however.

Despite the public outcry over the 1969 bombing of Cambodia, President Nixon decided, in the spring of 1970 that it was necessary for the United States to invade Cambodia to destroy supply bases and routes that were being used by the North Vietnamese. This time he announced the decision pub-licly. Many people thought he had made the wrong decision, and the protests and demonstrations grew.

Students on college campuses were especially active in opposing the president. Some of them forced their schools to shut down for short periods in protest of the war. Other dem-onstrations were violent, with youths throwing rocks and bot-tles at the police. In some places members of the National Guard—part-time citizen soldiers—were called in to restore order to the campuses.

On May 4, 1970, some members of the Ohio National Guard fired into a crowd of demonstrating students at Kent State University, killing four of them. This tragic incident caused a national uproar. Thousands and thousands of stu-dents marched on Washington to protest the killings and the continuing war.

President Nixon was troubled by the outpouring of hatred toward him. He also was angry at the chaos and vio-lence that occurred during some of the demonstrations. He decided to try and find out in advance what the antiwar groups were planning. To do this he needed some people to do intelligence—undercover—work.

The president was dissatisfied with the intelligence work already being done, so he asked the White House staff to come up with something better. The job was given to Tom Charles Huston, a young White House aide who earlier had worked in intelligence with the army. Huston met with leaders of the government agencies that specialize in secret and undercover work—the Central Intelligence Agency (CIA), the Federal Bureau of Investigation (FBI), the National Security Agency (NSA), and the Defense Intelligence Agency (DIA).

These agencies put together a proposal to find out more about the antiwar movement. It became known as the Huston plan. This plan proposed all kinds of illegal activities, such as reading people's private mail, listening in on their phone conversations, and breaking into their homes and offices.

Even though all of these things clearly were against the law, President Nixon approved the Huston plan. So did the leaders of most of the intelligence agencies. Fortunately, not everyone went along with it. J. Edgar Hoover, the FBI director, opposed it, as did Attorney General John Mitchell, who was head of the Department of Justice. Because of their objections, the Huston plan was dropped.

But the White House did not give up its attempts to thwart the antiwar demonstrators. On April 24, 1971, half a million people held a mostly peaceful demonstration in Washington. More radical groups planned a follow-up demonstration nine days later. They called it "Mayday" and said they would try to "shut down the war machine," meaning the government.

The Mayday demonstration is remembered because of the number of people arrested—seven thousand. Among those arrested were many who had done nothing wrong. All but about twenty-four of the cases were thrown out of court. Judges later ruled that the way the demonstrators had been arrested was illegal.

President Nixon took great interest in the demonstration. He asked the White House lawyer, John Dean, for reports every half hour. Dean rode above the city in a helicopter with another top White House aide, John D. Ehrlichman, to see what was going on. The White House was closely involved with efforts to control the demonstrators.

In this atmosphere, all kinds of scary and illegal proposals came up at the White House. In the summer of 1971 a White House aide proposed firebombing a big research agency in Washington, the Brookings Institution, in an attempt to get some papers from a man suspected of leaking information the White House wanted to keep secret. That firebombing never occurred. But the White House did send agents to break into another man's office. This happened during an incident involving what were known as the Pentagon Papers.

On June 13, 1971, the *New York Times* began publishing a series of stories that detailed America's involvement in Vietnam under presidents Kennedy and Johnson. These reports, which contained information that had been kept secret for years, were given to the *New York Times* by a Pentagon official, Daniel Ellsberg, who had turned against the war.

Even though the Pentagon Papers did not include any information about President Nixon's conduct of the Vietnam War, he was furious that the information had been made public. He filed a court suit to try and stop publication, arguing that the Pentagon Papers disclosed information that could harm the nation. But the U.S. Supreme Court ruled against the president, deciding that no damage would be done to the United States if the information were made public. The Pentagon Papers continued to be published.

Despite that ruling, Ellsberg was charged with theft, conspiracy, and violating a law aimed at discouraging spies.

Still President Nixon was unhappy. He decided that the White House should do all it could to discredit Ellsberg and teach him a lesson. And he made a new effort to stop leaks from government employees to the press. He told one of his aides, H. R. "Bob" Haldeman, to call in all of the top men in the government agencies and warn them that they could lose their jobs if the leaks did not stop. "You're going to be my lord high executioner from now on," Nixon told Haldeman.

President Nixon told another aide, John Ehrlichman, to

set up a special group in the White House to do undercover work. These men, who worked out of the White House basement, became known as "the Plumbers" because their job was to plug the "leaks."

Two of the people hired to work with the Plumbers later became key figures in the Watergate break-in. They were Howard Hunt, a former CIA agent, and G. Gordon Liddy, a former FBI man. Their main job while working with the Plumbers was to discredit Daniel Ellsberg.

The following conversation was recorded in July 1971 between Howard Hunt and White House aide Charles W. Colson:

COLSON: Let me ask you, Howard, this question: Do you think with the right resources employed, that this thing could be turned into a major public case against Ellsberg and coconspirators?
HUNT: Yes, I do. . . .
COLSON: Then your answer would be we should go down the line to nail the guy cold?
HUNT: Go down the line to nail the guy cold, yes.

White House officials had heard rumors that Ellsberg used illegal drugs and that he had consulted a psychiatrist. They decided to try and get information on Ellsberg from his psychiatrist, Dr. Lewis Fielding. It is considered unethical for any doctor, including psychiatrists, to reveal information about someone in their care. So naturally, Fielding refused when he was asked to hand over Ellsberg's private records.

This refusal did not deter the Plumbers, however. They decided that if Dr. Fielding would not give them the information on Daniel Ellsberg, then they would break into the psychiatrist's office and steal the information.

The break-in occurred in the first week of September 1971. Howard Hunt flew to Miami and recruited three men—Bernard Barker, Eugenio Martinez, and Felipe de Diego—to do the dirty work. Barker and Martinez would be used again later, during the Watergate burglary.

In the Ellsberg case, the burglars did not find what they

were looking for. The file was not in the psychiatrist's office. But John Ehrlichman, one of President Nixon's top aides, later went to prison for approving the break-in and for lying about it, or committing perjury, when a federal grand jury questioned him about it.

Despite the disappointing results of the break-in at Fielding's office, the team that had been assembled to discredit Ellsberg grew in influence. Nixon continuously pressed White House aides to get more information on his "enemies," so in the fall of 1971, with the 1972 presidential election just a year away, Hunt and Liddy joined the Committee for the Re-election of the President. Now they would begin practicing their dirty tricks on President Nixon's Democratic opponents.

3

POLITICAL SABOTAGE

PRESIDENT NIXON WAS WORRIED ABOUT BEING REELECTED in 1971. The Vietnam War and an inflationary economy both had cut into his popularity. When pollsters asked Americans who they were most likely to vote for in the 1972 election, they constantly picked Senator Edmund Muskie, a Democrat, over Nixon.

So in May 1971, a year and a half before the election, the president set up the Committee for the Re-election of the President, or CRP (known to Nixon's opposition as "Creep"). His campaign aides started planning ways to undermine Muskie and other men who were seeking the Democratic presidential nomination.

A spy was sent in to apply for a job with Muskie. He became Muskie's chauffeur, and reported back to the Nixon campaign on what he heard in the car.

When Muskie held a dinner at a hotel to try and raise money for his campaign, someone interrupted it with the delivery of pizzas, liquor, flowers, and cakes that Muskie had not ordered. Nixon workers had secretly placed the order and sent it C.O.D., cash on delivery.

Early in 1972, during the primary campaign in New Hampshire, voters were awakened in the middle of the night by callers who identified themselves as black youths from

Harlem. They said they were working for Muskie and asked the people in New Hampshire to vote for him. The effect was to make the voters angry with Muskie, just as the Nixon forces had planned.

At about the same time, a letter appeared in a newspaper in New Hampshire that falsely accused Muskie of making fun of a particular ethnic group, Americans who came from French-speaking Canada. A lot of voters in New Hampshire were members of that ethnic group, and they too became angry with Muskie.

Nixon campaign workers also made up stationery with Muskie's name on it and used it to write letters accusing two other Democratic presidential candidates of having sexual affairs. The charges were not true, but it looked as though Muskie was trying to make the two men look bad.

President Nixon was not necessarily aware of all of the dirty tricks his campaign workers performed on his behalf. But the victims blamed the man in charge at the White House.

Muskie told a *Washington Post* newspaper reporter, after he dropped out of the race, that his campaign had been hit with all kinds of sabotage. "Somebody was out to ambush us," Muskie said. "We assumed it was being done by Nixon people because that's the nature of this administration; they have no sensitivity to privacy or decency in politics. But we have no proof it was them."

The Nixon campaign also took aim at other potential Democratic presidential candidates. One man they feared, because he was popular in some parts of the country, was Senator Edward Kennedy of Massachusetts, brother of John F. and Robert Kennedy. Nixon aides spent a lot of time trying to dig up information to discredit Senator Kennedy.

Sometimes their efforts were just plain silly. Howard Hunt, hired as an undercover agent by the White House, wanted to talk to a man who supposedly had damaging information about Senator Kennedy. But Hunt did not want the man to know who he was, so he wore a wig and glasses and used a false name. He also had a device that made his voice sound different.

Nixon campaign workers often used code names for their

operations. They called their program to harass the Democrats "Sedan Chair," which came from a military exercise used by the U.S. Marines.

These secret harassment programs set the tone of the campaign. So it was not surprising to some Nixon aides when the proposals went from distasteful to illegal.

Officials at the CRP were under pressure from the White House to come up with more information about Nixon's opponents and to do more to disrupt the Democrats' campaign. They asked G. Gordon Liddy, who had worked with Hunt on the Ellsberg break-in, to devise a plan.

Liddy was a strange man. He turned up one day with a big white bandage around his fist. When people asked him what had happened, he said that to prove how brave he was, he had held his hand over a candle until his flesh burned.

Another time Liddy was having an argument with a campaign official and the official put his arm on Liddy's shoulder. "Get your hand off me," Liddy said loudly. "Get your hand off me or I'll kill you."

Even though White House officials knew Liddy was unusual, they thought he would be useful in planning the kind of operations they had in mind.

In January 1972 Liddy presented his plan for sabotaging the Democrats. The first part of the plan was designed to make sure that antiwar demonstrators did not disrupt the Republican presidential nominating convention, planned for August of that year. Liddy proposed kidnapping some of the antiwar leaders to keep them away from the convention. He said the leaders could be drugged and smuggled to a safe house in Mexico until after the convention. He also wanted to hire undercover agents to beat up other demonstrators.

Liddy had different plans for the Democratic convention, which was to be held in Miami that summer. He wanted to destroy the air-conditioning in the convention hall so that the hall would become stifling hot and the Democrats would look sweaty and uncomfortable on TV. He also proposed hiring prostitutes to work at the convention. They would try to lure prominent Democrats onto a "pleasure boat" and get them into embarrassing sexual situations. The boat would have hidden cameras and microphones to record everything.

Finally Liddy proposed a wiretapping program. One unusual aspect involved listening in on the conversations of Democratic presidential candidates while they traveled in private airplanes. He said he had bugging equipment that would allow the conversations to be heard from a "chase plane" that would follow the candidate's plane.

Liddy had names for each part of the secret plan—Operation Crystal, Operation Diamond, Operation Sapphire. The overall name would be Gemstone. He asked for $1 million in campaign money to carry it out.

Liddy presented this plan to former Attorney General John Mitchell, the head of the CRP, and John Dean, the White House lawyer. They rejected it, asking him to eliminate such ideas as kidnapping, using prostitutes, and sending chase planes after Democratic candidates.

So Liddy came up with another plan. This one, which called for spending $250,000, was approved by Mitchell in March 1972. It called for wiretapping the telephones of some of President Nixon's opponents. The campaign officials decided to start with Larry O'Brien, the Democratic party chairman, whose headquarters was at the Watergate.

Years later, after most of the information about Watergate became public, many people had trouble understanding why Nixon campaign officials had picked O'Brien as the first target.

Some thought it was because the White House was worried that Senator Kennedy might get into the Democratic presidential race. They knew that O'Brien was close to Kennedy and might have information about his plans. Others thought it was because O'Brien had been accusing Mitchell and other top Republicans of taking bribes in return for doing a favor for a big telephone company. Also, many Republicans thought O'Brien himself was involved in questionable activities, and they wanted to embarrass him.

Whatever the reasons, the decision was made in March 1972. The first break-in at O'Brien's Watergate office was done secretly and successfully on May 28, 1972. Bugs were put on the phones of O'Brien's secretary and one of his aides. But the Nixon campaign was not satisfied with the information it had received from these listening devices, and it was decided that another bug should be installed on O'Brien's telephone line.

This time the burglars were caught.

The White House could have accepted responsibility for the break-in, apologized, and possibly ended the entire episode. But it did not.

The cover-up was set in motion.

4

THE COVER-UP
BEGINS

PRESIDENT NIXON WAS VACATIONING IN THE BAHAMAS when the Watergate burglary occurred. Several of his top aides were in Key Biscayne, Florida, and the leaders of the CRP were in Los Angeles.

No matter where they were, the top officials at the White House and the reelection committee learned about the break-in within forty-eight hours after it occurred—that is, those who did not know about it beforehand.

No one suggested admitting that it was a White House operation. They wanted to keep it secret, fearing that if the public learned that top Republican officials were behind the burglary, there also might be revelations about the Ellsberg break-in and other political dirty tricks. President Nixon might not win reelection. It seemed to the men at the White House and the reelection committee that they could keep everything under wraps.

While the story had made the newspapers, most Americans were not very interested in the Watergate burglary right away. It did not seem important and a lot about it was unclear.

But the story did not die out. Reporters in Washington were interested because of the people involved and the unusual nature of the crime. They began investigating.

Democrats were eager to find out more as well, since they

hoped a story might develop that would help McGovern, their presidential candidate. But early on, they were no more successful in digging up information than the reporters were. The White House made sure of that.

The day of the break-in was a Saturday, and top officials of the CRP were in Los Angeles to attend a party with famous people who supported Nixon's bid for a second term in the White House.

Jeb Stuart Magruder, a top CRP official, was having breakfast in Los Angeles with other committee aides when he got a phone call from Liddy, the man who had planned the break-in. Liddy told Magruder that his men had been caught during the burglary at the Democratic headquarters in the Watergate. He also said that one of those arrested and taken to jail was James McCord, who worked directly for the reelection committee. That meant the break-in could be linked publicly to the committee right away.

Magruder was worried. He and another committee aide, Frederick LaRue, met with John Mitchell. They thought that if they could whisk McCord away, maybe no one would find out that he was connected to the reelection committee.

But McCord already was in jail in Washington, and they were in Los Angeles. How would they get McCord out of jail?

The men on the reelection committee decided to telephone the top law enforcement official in the nation, Attorney General Richard G. Kleindienst, and ask for his help. He would be able to free McCord.

When they telephoned Kleindienst's office, however, they were told that the attorney general was out playing golf. So they ordered Liddy to try to find him and make the request.

Liddy was able to find Kleindienst on the golf course, but the attorney general refused to talk to him and later exploded in anger at White House officials for putting him in such a position. McCord would not be freed. The first step in the Watergate cover-up had failed.

Although the top officials of the reelection committee were worried about the break-in, they did not let on to anyone else that they were upset. They went to a big Hollywood party that night with a lot of old-time movie stars—John Wayne, Zsa

Zsa Gabor, Charlton Heston, John Gavin, and Ronald Reagan, then governor of California. But even as they partied, some of the officials realized they were involved in a crime that could send them to jail.

Back in Washington, the first top aide to President Nixon to get news of the break-in was John Ehrlichman. A Secret Service agent called to tell him that one of the jailed burglars carried a notebook that had the name of a White House employee in it: E. Howard Hunt.

So now there were two links between the break-in and the White House—James McCord, security coordinator for the CRP, and Howard Hunt, who had an office in the White House. A third link was soon added—one hundred–dollar bills that the police found on the burglars were traced back to people who had made political donations to President Nixon's reelection committee.

Soon all of the top White House officials had been informed of what had happened:

• President Nixon was in the Bahamas with a millionaire friend, Robert Abplanalp, when the break-in occurred. The president flew to his home in Key Biscayne, Florida, on Sunday and read about the break-in in the newspaper. He telephoned two of his top aides that day, Bob Haldeman, the White House chief of staff, and Charles Colson, described by Haldeman as the president's personal hit man, the one who carried out all of the political dirty tricks. Colson later said that when Nixon learned of the break-in, he was so angry that he threw an ashtray across the room in his Key Biscayne home.

• Haldeman had learned about the break-in on Saturday while at the beach in Key Biscayne. White House Press Secretary Ronald L. Ziegler had brought him the news from a wire service machine. Haldeman, as Nixon's chief of staff, ran the White House with an iron fist. Other aides jumped whenever he gave an order.

• When Nixon spoke with Haldeman, he told Haldeman to telephone the CRP's Jeb Magruder in

Los Angeles to see what he knew about the break-in. Haldeman found Magruder very nervous when he called.

• John Dean, the White House lawyer, was flying back to Washington from the Philippines when his assistant, Fred Fielding, got hold of him and described the break-in. Fielding told Dean he should hurry back to Washington. Dean had sat in on the meetings at the reelection committee where G. Gordon Liddy was given the go-ahead to tap telephones and perform other political dirty tricks. And it was Dean who had assigned Liddy to work with the reelection committee.

On the Monday morning after the break-in, Dean had a meeting with Liddy to find out just what had happened. They went for a walk and sat down to talk in a park near the White House.

According to Dean, Liddy took responsibility for the fact that the burglars had been caught, saying the foul-up occurred because he had been pushed by Jeb Magruder to do the job too fast with too little money. That was why he had used James McCord, a man who so easily could be linked to the reelection committee, instead of someone who would have been harder to trace back to the president's men. Liddy said he had not been given enough time to do the break-in properly.

Liddy said something else that shocked Dean during their meeting in the park. He said if it would help, he was ready to be shot to death. Dean told him it would not be necessary. Liddy then vowed that none of the burglars would reveal the truth about Watergate. The two men parted.

In the days that followed, the White House and the reelection committee moved swiftly to try to keep damage from the Watergate break-in from spreading. Papers related to political tricks were taken out of the files and destroyed. A safe that Howard Hunt kept in his office at the White House was opened and the contents, including a revolver, were locked away for awhile and then finally were given to L. Patrick Gray, Jr., the temporary director of the FBI. Gray destroyed the documents, even though it is against the law to destroy evidence that relates to a criminal investigation.

There was an investigation of the Watergate break-in—by the FBI itself, so it amounted to the fox guarding the henhouse.

Not long before the break-in, the longtime director of the FBI, J. Edgar Hoover, had died. President Nixon chose Pat Gray as his replacement. Gray had worked for Nixon when he ran for president unsuccessfully in 1960.

When the break-in occurred, Gray was acting FBI director, meaning that he had been chosen by the president for the job but the Senate had not yet agreed to the choice.

Gray was eager to please the president, and he went along with the White House when it asked him to take the documents from Hunt's safe, to limit the investigation of the break-in, and to keep the White House informed of the probe every step of the way. Gray allowed John Dean to sit in on interviews with people the FBI talked with to get information on the case.

Even President Nixon was involved in the effort to keep FBI agents from finding out too much. When the agents started asking questions about things the White House wanted kept secret, Haldeman suggested a plan to the president. Haldeman said that Vernon Walters, deputy director of the CIA and a longtime friend of Nixon's, should be asked to tell Gray that the agents should limit their investigation so that they would not stumble into areas involving national security.

National security is a term used to describe information that is important to the safety and well-being of America, information that could cause the country harm if other nations learned about it. The CIA, in its role as undercover agent for the United States, has many national security secrets. In the Watergate case, no such secrets were involved. But Haldeman knew that if a top CIA official told Gray that national security was at stake, Gray would limit the Watergate investigation.

On June 23, 1972, about a week after the break-in, Haldeman discussed this idea with Nixon at the White House. "Now on the investigation, you know, the Democratic break-in thing, we're back in the problem area," Haldeman said to the president, indicating that the two had discussed the break-in before. "The FBI is not under control because Gray doesn't exactly know how to control it and they have—their investigation is now leading into some problem areas."

He explained that other White House aides had discussed the FBI problem and concluded that "the way to handle this now is for us to have Walters call Pat Gray and just say, 'stay the hell out of this—this is business here we don't want you to go any further on it.' That's not an unusual development, and that would take care of it." After some discussion of alternatives, Haldeman told the president, "They'll [the FBI investigators] stop if we could take this other route."

"All right," the president replied.

"And you seem to think the thing to do is get them to stop?" Haldeman asked, meaning using the CIA to get the FBI to limit its investigation.

"Right, fine," Nixon replied.

A little later in the conversation, Nixon added, "Of course this [E. Howard] Hunt, that will uncover a lot of things. You open that scab, there's a hell of a lot of things, and we just feel that it would be very detrimental to have this thing go any further. This involves these Cubans, Hunt and a lot of hanky-panky that we have nothing to do with ourselves. Well, what the hell, did Mitchell know about this?"

"I think so," Haldeman replied. "I don't think he knew the details, but I think he knew."

Nixon then said, "He didn't know how it was going to be handled, though. . . . Well who was the asshole that did? Is it Liddy? Is that the fellow? He must be a little nuts."

"He is," said Haldeman.

Nixon added, "I mean, he just isn't well screwed on, is he? Is that the problem?"

Haldeman said, "No, but he was under pressure, apparently to get information, and as he got more pressure, he pushed the people harder to move harder. . . ."

"Pressure from Mitchell?" Nixon asked.

"Apparently," Haldeman said.

"All right, fine," Nixon said. "We won't second-guess Mitchell and the rest."

In this conversation, Nixon gave approval to the plan to short-circuit the FBI investigation by using the CIA, and he acknowledged that he knew that one of his top aides, John Mitchell, was involved in the break-in.

This conversation would come back to haunt the president. But in June 1972 no one outside the room was aware of this important discussion.

As it turned out, Walters did talk to Gray, asking him to hold off on the investigation until Walters could see whether any national security secrets were involved. But several days later Walters told Gray that no national security secrets were at stake, and he resisted further White House pressure to try to limit the FBI investigation.

In the final week of June, the White House and the re-election committee also began arranging to make payments to the Watergate burglars to help pay their legal costs and to support their families while the men were in jail.

These payments were highly secretive, since anyone learning about them would think the White House was paying hush money to the burglars—that is, money to ensure that the burglars did not reveal that they were working for the president's men.

To arrange the payments, John Dean met with another lawyer, Herbert Kalmbach, on a park bench to discuss the matter, just as spies meet outdoors to make sure that no one is listening to their conversations.

Over the next three months the White House would funnel $220,000 to the burglars through secret meetings. At the end of the summer it appeared that the cover-up was working.

5

REPORTERS STALK THE WATERGATE STORY

DURING THE SUMMER AFTER THE WATERGATE BREAK-IN, the public knew almost nothing about what was going on behind the scenes.

The break-in was reported in the newspapers, the Justice Department began an investigation, and a federal grand jury was convened to hear evidence in the case and decide whether anyone should be brought to trial. But the prosecutors focused on the five men who had been caught red-handed in the Democratic national headquarters. There was no evidence yet that the break-in involved anyone in the White House.

On August 23 Richard Nixon was nominated to run for a second term as president by the Republican party at its national convention in Miami. A week later, at a news conference, Nixon was asked about the break-in. He said that the White House lawyer, John Dean, had conducted an investigation of Watergate and added:

> I can state categorically that his investigation indicates that no one on the White House staff, no one in this administration, presently employed, was involved in this very bizarre incident. What really hurts in matters of this sort is not the fact that they

occur, because overzealous people in campaigns do things that are wrong. What really hurts is if you try to cover it up.

Although the president announced that John Dean had investigated the Watergate break-in, this was untrue. Dean later revealed that the first he had heard about the investigation he supposedly had conducted was when Nixon announced it on television.

In early September the Justice Department finished its investigation of the break-in, and on September 15, 1972, the federal grand jury that had listened to evidence in the case returned an indictment against the five burglars—McCord, the man who had worked as security coordinator for the reelection committee, Barker, Sturgis, Gonzalez, and Martinez. In addition, the grand jury indicted the two men found skulking around the Watergate the night of the break-in—Liddy and Hunt.

All seven men were charged with illegally tapping telephones, installing eavesdropping equipment at the Democratic headquarters, and stealing papers from the office.

A grand jury is simply a group of citizens chosen at random by the government to help in the legal process. People chosen for the grand jury report each day to a government building. When the Justice Department thinks someone is guilty of a crime, it presents its evidence to the grand jury. Members of the grand jury then decide if they think the government's case against the person is strong enough to require a trial.

If the grand jurors agree with the prosecutors that the person should stand trial, the person is formally charged with the crime and told that he or she has the right to a trial. The charges are written up in a document called an indictment.

Once the Justice Department obtained indictments against the Watergate burglars, it concluded that it did not need to look any further to see who else might be involved. "We have absolutely no evidence to indicate that any others should be charged," a Justice Department official told reporters.

Attorney General Richard Kleindienst, the top man at the Justice Department, said that the probe into Watergate was "one of the most intensive, objective and thorough investigations in many years, reaching out to cities all across the United States as well as into foreign countries."

But many reporters and some members of Congress felt that there was much more to the Watergate story than had been revealed so far.

Editors at the *Washington Post* assigned two reporters to the story full-time—Bob Woodward and Carl Bernstein.

Woodward, who was twenty-nine at the time, and Bernstein, twenty-eight, both were very ambitious. Neither man was married and they had no children, so they were able to spend a lot of time working. When they got assigned to the Watergate story, they began working even harder.

Their work paid off. On August 1, 1972, Woodward and Bernstein reported one of the first major stories on the Watergate break-in. They had discovered the money link between the burglars and the Nixon reelection committee.

Specifically, they found out that $25,000 collected in the Midwest for President Nixon's reelection campaign had been deposited into the bank account of Bernard Barker, one of the Miami men arrested in the break-in.

The man who had signed the check, Kenneth H. Dahlberg, was the Midwest finance chairman for the reelection committee. Dahlberg told Woodward that he had given the $25,000 check to Maurice H. Stans, Nixon's chief money-raiser, on April 11.

This was an important revelation because it established that money intended for the reelection campaign had instead ended up in the bank account of a Watergate burglar. When Stans was confronted with the story, he refused to comment on it. The reelection committee also had nothing to say.

The reporters followed up on the story by trying to find out more about the reelection committee's money. They eventually learned that Stans and others who worked for Nixon had secretly collected hundreds of thousands of dollars from people—many of them Democrats who disliked George

McGovern—who did not want it publicly known that they had given money to the Nixon campaign fund.

To keep the contributions secret, the reelection committee had sent the money across the U.S. border to Mexico, through the bank accounts of other people, and then back to Washington. Because the money had gone through so many channels, it could not be traced back to the original contributors. This process is called money laundering.

On August 26 a congressional agency, the General Accounting Office, said it believed that the Nixon reelection committee had violated a number of laws in the way it collected money for the president's campaign. It asked the Justice Department to investigate.

But a few weeks later, when Kleindienst announced the indictment of the Watergate burglars, no reference was made to the money or the illegal fund-raising. Reporters wondered why. They knew there was more to the story than had been revealed so far.

Woodward and Bernstein were able to convince a lot of people to talk to them secretly about what really was going on. At night they visited the homes of people who worked for the Nixon reelection committee. Many of the people were afraid they would lose their jobs if they talked with the reporters, but some were so disgusted with the Watergate break-in and other illegal activities that they talked anyway. A bookkeeper at the reelection committee helped, as did the committee treasurer, Hugh Sloan. Some FBI agents were willing to talk too. They knew that the investigation the Justice Department was doing was not very thorough.

Reporters at the other newspapers and magazines also got people to talk with them, and as time went on they were able to piece together more about the Watergate story. But Woodward and Bernstein got the most information, partly because of hard work, partly because they worked for the most powerful newspaper in Washington, and partly because Woodward had a source that no one else had.

The source worked in the Nixon administration and

knew what was going on at the White House, within the Nixon reelection committee, and at the Justice Department.

Because the man was in such a sensitive position, he did not want anyone to know he was talking to a *Washington Post* reporter, so Woodward was careful never to reveal his name. He did not even tell Bernstein or his editors who the man was. The editors accepted this because the man's information was always right. One of them gave him a code name, since they did not know his real name.

He became known as Deep Throat.

Woodward has never publicly revealed the identity of this special source. Some people believe that Deep Throat actually was two or three people, but that is only a guess.

Woodward did not meet with Deep Throat in restaurants, at the office, or in other public places, and they almost never talked on the phone for fear that the phones might be bugged. Instead they met in the middle of the night in an underground garage.

Woodward lived in a high-rise apartment that had a balcony. Whenever he wanted to talk with Deep Throat, he moved a flowerpot from the front of his balcony to the back. That was the signal for a middle-of-the-night meeting in the underground garage.

To get to the meeting Woodward would catch a taxicab, then get out and find another cab and sometimes a third. Sometimes, when he could not find a cab, he would walk. He used these roundabout methods of travel to make sure that no one was following him.

Deep Throat told Woodward that he should watch his step. He said that the White House was upset about the stories in the *Post* and warned that the reporter's telephones could be bugged and that people might be watching him.

In late September the reporters learned firsthand just how angry their stories were making the Nixon men when they revealed secret information about John Mitchell.

Mitchell was a lawyer who had been attorney general before Kleindienst. He had quit that job to take over Nixon's reelection committee. Woodward and Bernstein learned that he had been in charge of a secret campaign fund at the reelection committee while he was still in his job as attorney general and that he had given approval for the money to be used to spy on Democratic politicians.

The story reflected badly on Mitchell because it is illegal for government officials to work for a political candidate while they are in office. That is especially true for the attorney general, since he is the top law enforcement agent in the nation.

The night before the *Post* published the story. Bernstein telephoned Mitchell to ask for his comment. He reached Mitchell at 11:30 P.M. and found him extremely angry.

"All that crap, you're putting it in the paper?" Mitchell said. "It's all been denied. Katie Graham [publisher of the *Washington Post*] is gonna get her tit caught in a big fat wringer if that's published. Good Christ. That's the most sickening thing I ever heard."

Bernstein told Mitchell that while the reelection committee had issued a statement about the story, he wanted to ask Mitchell a few specific questions.

"Did the committee tell you to go ahead and publish that story?" Mitchell replied. "You fellows got a great ballgame going. As soon as you're through paying Ed Williams [the *Post*'s lawyer] and the rest of those fellows, we're going to do a story on all of you."

The last statement was an indirect threat. It meant that the Nixon administration would try to get even with the *Post* for the stories it was doing.

The newspaper included Mitchell's quotes in its story, all except the words *her tit*.

On October 24, Woodward and Bernstein wrote a story saying that Bob Haldeman was another person who had controlled the secret money fund that was used to sabotage the Democrats. With this story they had upped the ante—Haldeman was perhaps the man closest in the White House to Richard Nixon.

While the story was true, Woodward and Bernstein had made a key mistake. They reported that Hugh Sloan, the former treasurer for the Nixon reelection committee, had told the grand jury investigating Watergate that Haldeman was in charge of the secret fund.

Sloan had *not* told the grand jury about Haldeman, simply because he had not been asked about him. But neither the reporters nor the public knew this. They knew only that Sloan was denying the *Post* story.

The mistake was greeted with glee at the White House and the *Post* was widely criticized for the story. The reporters, demoralized, tried to piece together what had gone wrong with their story.

A couple of weeks later Richard Nixon won reelection to the White House. He won a majority of votes in every state except Massachusetts and in the District of Columbia.

It was clear that most people were unconcerned about Watergate as 1972 drew to a close. But all of that would change in the year that followed.

6

THE BURGLARY
TRIAL

THE TRIAL OF THE WATERGATE BURGLARS BEGAN ON JANU-
ary 8, 1973. John Sirica, chief judge of the U.S. District Court
presided in a high-ceilinged ceremonial courtroom that added
to the drama.

Every seat was filled as the Justice Department prosecutor, Earl Silbert, began to speak after two days of jury se-
lection. It was Silbert's job to outline for the jury the case
against the burglars.

Silbert told the jury what officials at the Nixon reelection
committee had told him—that G. Gordon Liddy was the boss
in charge of the break-in. Silbert said that the reelection committee had given Liddy a lot of money—$235,000—to use for
legitimate political activities, and that instead Liddy had used
the money for the illegal break-in and other improper projects.

Why had the defendants broken into the Watergate offices of the Democratic National Committee? "Obviously it
was a political motive, political campaign," Silbert explained.
"The operation was directed against the Democratic Party,
particularly Senator George McGovern because of his alleged
left-wing views."

But, Silbert said, not all of the Watergate burglars had
had the same motive. "The motivation of the defendant Hunt
and defendant Liddy may have been different from the motiva-

tions of the four defendants from Miami, and they in turn may have had a different motivation than defendant McCord."

Silbert suggested that McCord and the four Miami men had joined in simply for the money they received from Liddy and Hunt for doing the job. "It was a financial motive," he said.

When Silbert finished speaking, the lawyers for the defendants got their turn to speak to the jury. McCord's lawyer, Gerald Alch, was first. He disputed Silbert's idea that McCord had joined the burglary for the money. "The evidence will not show that Mr. McCord was present at the Watergate on the night in question for any type of financial reward or gain," Alch said. "The existence of a criminal intent is a necessary ingredient of every crime. We will show that Mr. McCord had no criminal intent. We will show that Mr. McCord was not aware of all of those facts which might make his conduct criminal."

Next up was Henry Rothblatt, lawyer for the four Miami men. He too disputed Silbert's idea that money was the motive behind the break-in. He portrayed his clients as little guys with patriotic motives who had gotten caught up in something run by others. However, he did not say who was running the show.

The last lawyer to speak was William Bittman, representing E. Howard Hunt. Bittman offered no defense. Instead he said that his client wanted to plead guilty.

Judge Sirica did not want Hunt to leave the trial proceedings without shedding any light on the break-in, so he tried to get him to talk. "Now, in your own words, I would like you to tell me from the beginning just how you got into this conspiracy, what you did, various things that you did, so I can decide whether or not you are knowingly and intentionally entering this plea voluntarily with full knowledge of possible consequences," Sirica told Hunt.

But Hunt's attorney argued that the proper place for Hunt to discuss such matters was before the grand jury that was still hearing evidence in the Watergate case, not in open court.

Despite his desire to learn more about the real story of Watergate, Judge Sirica knew that Hunt's lawyer was legally correct, so he accepted Hunt's guilty plea without any exchange of information.

By the end of the first week of the trial, it was becoming apparent that none of the defendants was going to talk. The four Miami men now wanted to plead guilty, just as Hunt had done, but their lawyer would not agree because he felt that his clients were being pressured by Hunt to follow his example. The Miami men were determined, however, so they fired their lawyer and got a new one who went along with their wish.

In the days that followed, the *New York Times* reported that the four Miami men were being paid by someone to remain silent. Similar stories followed in the *Post, Time* magazine, and other publications.

In court, Judge Sirica asked the Miami men outright if they were being paid to remain silent. They all said no.

They also resisted the judge's attempts to get to the bottom of the case. When Sirica asked Barker, the leader of the four Miamians, where he had got the money to pay his colleagues, Barker replied, "Your honor, I got that money in the mail in a blank envelope."

"I'm sorry. I don't believe you," Judge Sirica replied. But he had to accept the guilty pleas, despite his misgivings. That left only Liddy and McCord as defendants in the case.

The trial pressed on, but little was revealed in the testimony. As would become clear later, several top officials from the reelection committee lied on the witness stand. When a witness lies in court, that is called perjury, a crime in itself.

Jeb Magruder, deputy director of the reelection committee, was the top official to testify at the trial. His answers had been carefully rehearsed. Although Magruder had sat in on the meeting where Liddy was given a go-ahead to break into the Watergate, he concealed this fact during his testimony.

"Mr. Magruder, did you ever give Mr. Liddy any assignment concerning the Democratic National Committee?" prosecutor Earl Silbert asked.

"No," Magruder replied.

"Did you ever receive any report of any kind from Mr. Liddy concerning the Democratic National Committee offices and headquarters?"

"No," Magruder said.

Other witnesses also stopped short whenever it seemed that anyone at the reelection committee might be implicated in the break-in.

Alfred Baldwin, the man who had worked with the Watergate burglars by serving as a lookout from the balcony of the Howard Johnson's, had agreed to testify for the prosecution.

He said that he had made written transcripts of the conversations he overheard on the bugged telephones at Democratic headquarters. And, he added, at one point McCord had instructed him to put the transcripts in an envelope and deliver them to a specific person on the reelection committee. But Baldwin said he could not remember the name of the person who was to receive the envelope.

Judge Sirica clearly thought that Baldwin had purposely "forgotten" the name of the person on the reelection committee.

"You wrote the name of that party, correct?" Sirica said.

"Yes, I did," Baldwin replied.

"On the envelope. You personally took that envelope to the Committee to Re-elect the President, correct?"

"Yes, I did," Baldwin answered.

"What is the name of that party?" the judge asked.

"I do not know, your honor," Baldwin said.

The testimony of other witnesses continued in the same manner. No one could remember anything that would get anyone at the reelection committee in trouble.

Although all of the defendants said they had made their decisions to plead guilty—and not to talk—independently, a different story was being unveiled at the White House.

Hunt, through his lawyer, had been putting pressure on the White House for more money to support the Watergate defendants and their families in return for their loyal silence.

He had spoken directly to his old White House boss, Charles Colson, about money for the defendants in a phone conversation the previous November. Colson had tape-recorded the conversation:

HUNT: There's a great deal of unease and concern on the part of the seven defendants . . . there's a great deal of financial expense that has not been covered and what we've been getting has been coming in very minor dribs and drabs . . . this is a long haul thing and the stakes are very high. And I thought that you would want to know that this thing must not break apart for foolish reasons.

Hunt also wanted assurances that if he pleaded guilty, he would not have to spend years in jail. In January, when he was about to go on trial, he again tried to press his case with Colson.

Colson, feeling the pressure, had a discussion with President Nixon in January 1973 about the Watergate defendants' agreement to remain silent at the trial and about the possibility of clemency—a presidential order freeing the men from jail after they were convicted.

NIXON: Well, first of all they've got to make a production in Liddy's case. But none of them are going to testify. Isn't that correct? You know, Chuck, it's something they all undertook knowing the risks. Right? What do you think?

COLSON: I don't think there's any doubt about it.

Then the two turned to the question of clemency.

NIXON: Basically I question clemency. Hunt's is a simple case. I mean, after all, the man's wife is dead, was killed; he's got one child that has . . .

COLSON: Brain damage from an automobile accident.

Nixon then begins to consider how clemency for Hunt could be made politically acceptable. He proposed that the White House get a newspaper columnist to write in favor of clemency for Hunt.

NIXON: We'll build that son of a bitch [Hunt] up like nobody's business . . . We'll talk about it after. That's it. It's on the merits.

But of course, neither the judge nor the jury nor the public was aware at the time what was going on behind the scenes at the White House.

And nothing so dramatic as this conversation came out during the sixteen-day trial. Neither Liddy nor McCord testified in his own defense, and the jury convicted both of them after just ninety minutes of deliberation on January 30, 1973.

A few days after the verdict, when Judge Sirica had the defendants back in court for a hearing, he made clear that he was not pleased with the outcome.

"I have not been satisfied that all the pertinent facts that might be available—I say might be available—have been produced before an American jury," Sirica said. He noted that Congress was not satisfied with the matter either and planned to hold hearings in the next few months. "I would frankly hope, not only as a judge but as a citizen of a great country and one of millions of Americans who are looking for certain answers, I would hope that the Senate committee is granted the power by Congress by a broad enough resolution to try to get to the bottom of what happened in this case."

He would not have long to wait. Within the following two months, the entire Watergate cover-up would begin to unravel.

7

"A CANCER ON THE PRESIDENCY"

IN FEBRUARY 1973 SEVERAL THINGS HAPPENED THAT MADE the White House nervous. First, the Senate voted unanimously to set up a special committee to delve into the continuing mysteries of Watergate. It began hiring lawyers in preparation for public hearings that would start the following summer.

Then Patrick Gray, acting director of the FBI since the death of J. Edgar Hoover, was nominated by President Nixon to get the job permanently. Before that could happen, however, the Senate had to give its approval. And the Senate was not about to approve the nomination until it had questioned Gray about the FBI's investigation of Watergate.

While the White House said publicly that it would cooperate in the hearings, John Dean, the president's lawyer, testified later that the private strategy of the president's men was different. What the White House would secretly try to do, Dean said, was "attempt to restrain the investigation and make it as difficult as possible to get information and witnesses. . . . The ultimate goal would be to discredit the hearings."

But the more immediate problem for the White House was the Gray confirmation hearings, which began on February 28. To the amazement and disgust of the White House, Gray revealed to the Senate that John Dean had sat in on interviews the FBI conducted during the Watergate investigation. Gray also told the senators that Dean had received copies of the reports the FBI made during its investigation.

Many senators thought that this cozy arrangement between Dean and the FBI was wrong. After all, the FBI had been investigating the Nixon reelection committee. And Dean, as Nixon's lawyer, had a direct interest in seeing that the FBI did not implicate anyone on the reelection committee—or in the White House—in the Watergate burglary.

The senators decided to ask Dean to testify on Capitol Hill. But President Nixon refused to allow his lawyer to appear before the Senate and said that other top members of his staff would not agree to testify either.

Under the American form of government, with its three branches, the executive branch—the White House—has the right to keep some information secret. This is called executive privilege.

Many thought that Nixon was abusing this privilege when he refused to let Dean testify, but the president argued that it was all for the good of the country: "Executive privilege will not be used as a shield to prevent embarrassing information from being made available but will be exercised only in those particular instances in which disclosure would harm the public interest," he said in a policy statement.

Of course this was not true, especially in Dean's case. The young White House lawyer had all kinds of information that could embarrass the president, and that was the reason Nixon did not want him to testify.

Dean was relieved that he would not have to be a witness at the Senate hearings, but at the same time he was growing more and more frustrated about his role in Watergate. While he had been secretly involved in the cover-up from the beginning, his name had not been before the public until Patrick Gray began testifying on Capitol Hill.

Now Dean's name was in newspaper headlines—"Dean Monitored FBI Watergate Probe," said one—he was under pressure from the Senate, and the continuing problems of Watergate were increasingly dumped on his lap.

In mid-March, shortly before he was to be sentenced to prison for his role in the Watergate break-in, Howard Hunt

sent a message directly to Dean. He wanted $120,000 imme-
diately or he would break the code of silence the burglars had
maintained thus far.

The Nixon reelection committee and the White House
already had given the Watergate burglars a lot of money. This
latest demand for hush money from Hunt made Dean realize
what a never-ending nightmare Watergate had become. These
money demands could go on forever. And everywhere he
looked, another problem cropped up. He knew the things he
had done could put him in jail.

With all this in mind, Dean decided to have a long talk
with the president. He later told investigators that his intention
was to force an end to the cover-up.

The president and Dean met in the Oval Office on March
21, 1973. They talked for almost two hours in what was to
become one of the most infamous conversations to come out
of Watergate.

DEAN: I think that there is no doubt about the seriousness of the
problem we've got. We have a cancer within, close to the presidency,
that is growing. It is growing daily. It's compounded, growing geo-
metrically now. . . . Basically, it is because (1) we are being black-
mailed; (2) people are going to start perjuring themselves very
quickly that have not had to perjure themselves to protect other people in the line. And there is no assurance . . .
NIXON: That that won't bust?
DEAN: That that won't bust [that someone in the chain of the cover-
up might reveal the truth].

Dean went on to outline for the president the origins of
the Watergate problem—how he had sent Liddy to the reelection committee, how Liddy had proposed a number of illegal
activities that had been rejected, and how Liddy had ultimately
proposed breaking into the Democratic party headquarters, an
illegal action that the reelection committee had approved. And
finally, Dean told Nixon about the continuing demands for
money from Howard Hunt.

DEAN: Hunt now is demanding another $72,000 for his own personal expenses; another $50,000 to pay attorney's fees—$120,000 . . . he wanted it as of the close of business yesterday. He said, "I am going to be sentenced on Friday and I've got to get my affairs in order." . . . Hunt has made a direct threat against Ehrlichman. As a result of this, this is his blackmail. He says, "I will bring John Ehrlichman down to his knees and put him in jail. I have done enough seamy things for him and [Egil] Krogh [an aide to Ehrlichman] they'll never survive it."

NIXON: Was he talking about Ellsberg [the September 1971 break-in authorized by Ehrlichman in an attempt to smear the man who leaked the Pentagon Papers]?

DEAN: Ellsberg and apparently some other things. I don't know the full extent of it.

NIXON: I don't know of anything else.

After some further discussion, Dean steered the conversation back to the problems of continuing the cover-up, especially the money sought by Hunt.

DEAN: First of all, there is the problem of the continued blackmail, which will not only go on now, but it will go on while these people are in prison and it will compound the obstruction of justice situation. It will cost money. It is dangerous. People around here are not pros at this sort of thing. This is the sort of thing Mafia people can do—washing money, getting clean money and things like that. We just don't know about those things because we are not criminals and not used to dealing in that business.

NIXON: That's right.

DEAN: It is a tough thing to know how to do.

NIXON: Maybe it takes a gang to do that.

DEAN: That's right. There is a real problem as to whether we could even do it. Plus there is a real problem in raising money. Mitchell has been working on raising some money. He is one of the ones with the most to lose. But there is no denying the fact that the White House, in Ehrlichman, Haldeman and Dean, are involved in some of the early money decisions.

At that point, Nixon turned to the most immediate problem the White House faced—getting the money to keep the burglars quiet.

NIXON: How much money do you need?

DEAN: I would say these people are going to cost a million dollars over the next two years.

NIXON: We could get that. On the money, if you need the money you could get that. You could get a million dollars. You could get it in cash. I know where it could be gotten. It is not easy, but it could be done.

As the talk continued, Dean explained to Nixon that if the cover-up were to end, some people probably would go to jail—including Dean himself. Dean said he could be accused of obstruction of justice, meaning that he had known about a crime and had helped cover it up.

NIXON: Talking about your obstruction of justice though, I don't see it.

DEAN: Well, I have been a conduit for information on taking care of people out there who are guilty of crimes.

NIXON: Oh, you mean like the blackmailers?

DEAN: The blackmailers. Right.

NIXON: Well, I wonder if that part of it can't be—I wonder if that doesn't—let me put if frankly: I wonder if that doesn't have to be continued. Let me put it this way. Let us suppose that you get the million bucks, and you get the proper way to handle it. You could hold that side [keep the burglars quiet]?

DEAN: Uh huh.

NIXON: It would seem to me that would be worthwhile.

Dean got the message. That night, $75,000 was put into a plain envelope and delivered to Howard Hunt's attorney. That would keep Hunt quiet for awhile.

Aside from the immediate problem of the hush money, Dean thought the president might benefit by saying publicly that he had recently received new information about Watergate and then request that a new grand jury be impaneled to look into the information. That way, Dean argued, some people would have to go to jail, but at least it would end the lies, the perjury, and the deepening involvement of the president in the cover-up.

Haldeman joined the conversation eventually, and the three discussed the problem further. They did not reach a definite conclusion.

That evening, however, another meeting was held and John Ehrlichman joined in. He made it clear from the outset that he was opposed to the idea of ending the cover-up. The final blow was struck the next day, March 22, during a meeting of Nixon, Haldeman, Ehrlichman, Mitchell, and Dean.

NIXON: Do you think we want to go this route now? Let it all hang out so to speak?
DEAN: Well, it isn't really that . . .
HALDEMAN: It is a limited hangout. It's not an absolute hang out.
NIXON: But some of the questions look big hanging out, privately or publicly.
DEAN: But what it is doing, Mr. President, is getting you up and away from it. That is the most important thing.
NIXON: Oh, I know. I suggested that the other day and they [Haldeman and Ehrlichman] all came down negative on it. Now what has changed their minds?
DEAN: Lack of a candidate or a body.

Everyone laughed at this point. What Dean meant was that no one was willing to take the rap for Watergate, to go to jail to save the others.

So the hours of discussion had been for nothing. The White House would continue to stonewall.

But John Dean was right. Watergate was like a cancer on the presidency. Despite all attempts to contain it, new problems were appearing regularly.

Burglar James W. McCord, Jr., was the next one.

8

THE COVER-UP
FALLS APART

IN MARCH AND APRIL 1973, THE WATERGATE COVER-UP FELL apart. Here's what happened:

- One of the Watergate burglars talked, implicating both John Dean (the president's lawyer) and Jeb Magruder (a top reelection committee official) in the Watergate affair.
- In hopes of avoiding a jail term, John Dean decided to get a criminal lawyer and tell the true story of Watergate to federal prosecutors.
- Jeb Magruder also decided to tell the truth and admitted he had lied at the trial of the Watergate burglars.
- Patrick Gray resigned as acting director of the FBI when it was revealed that he had burned some of E. Howard Hunt's papers in an attempt to cover up Watergate.
- Dean and Magruder told the prosecutors that the president's two top aides, Bob Haldeman and John Ehrlichman, were involved in the Watergate cover-up.
- Nixon fired Dean and accepted the resignations of Haldeman and Ehrlichman.

The first major blow to the cover-up came from James McCord. McCord had worked for the CIA for nineteen years

and later for the Nixon reelection committee. G. Gordon
Liddy had asked him to take part in the Watergate burglary
because he needed to find someone dependable fast.

Since his arrest in June 1972, McCord had honored the
code of silence among the Watergate defendants, hiding the
fact that top Republican officials had authorized the break-in.
But he had made it clear that he was unhappy about having to
take the rap while others involved, such as John Dean and Jeb
Magruder, went free. "This was not my idea of American justice," he said.

White House officials tried to convince McCord to go
along with the other burglars. They sent an aide to meet with
him secretly. The aide promised that if McCord went to
prison, his family would be taken care of and he would have a
job waiting for him when he got out.

But McCord was not swayed by such promises and was
incensed when Magruder falsely testified at the burglars' trial
that no higher officials were involved. McCord decided that
before he was sentenced to prison, he would write a letter to
Judge Sirica.

On March 23 Sirica called all of the Watergate burglars
to court to impose jail sentences on them. Everyone was expecting a routine court hearing, but the judge had a surprise.
He read McCord's letter aloud in the courtroom.

McCord's letter revealed that
• Political pressure was applied to the defendants to
plead guilty and remain silent.
• Perjury occurred during the trial and it related to
important information.
• Others involved in the Watergate operation were
not identified during the trial, although they could
have been by those testifying.

The letter also revealed that McCord expected that he
would be punished for breaking the code of silence. "Several
members of my family have expressed fear for my life if I disclose knowledge of the facts in this matter," McCord wrote.
"Whereas I do not share their concerns to the same degree,
nevertheless, I do believe retaliatory measures will be taken
against me, my family and my friends should I disclose such

facts." Despite those fears, McCord said he had decided to talk.

The letter caused a sensation in the courtroom. Judge Sirica was so tense that he got horrible pains in his chest as he was reading and had to leave the courtroom to lie down as soon as he finished the letter. Reporters rushed out to give the news about McCord to their editors.

In the following days, McCord also talked to the lawyers working for the Senate Watergate Committee. He told them that both John Dean and Jeb Magruder had been involved in Watergate.

McCord's letter, coming on top of the recent testimony by the FBI's Gray, hastened a change in public perception about Watergate. Interest in the case intensified and polls showed that more people thought President Nixon had known about the break-in from the outset. "Honk if you think he's guilty," bumper stickers said. Reporters from newspapers, magazines, television, and radio competed to find out more about the scandal. Top Watergate figures awoke in the mornings to find TV reporters waiting outside their doors, eager to get a statement.

In this atmosphere, John Dean made a momentous decision. Under intense pressure and feeling ever surer that the cover-up was falling apart and that he would be made a scapegoat, he decided to get a lawyer and reveal the true story of Watergate.

Dean would pay dearly for his decision. He would be pitted directly against the president, vilified by the White House, and considered a squealer and a liar by large numbers of Americans.

But he did not know any of that when he made his decision. He hired criminal lawyer Charles Shaffer and began spilling out details of Watergate, from the first meetings with Liddy to the scramble for money to keep the burglars quiet and to the most recent days in the White House and the attempt to keep everything under wraps.

Dean hoped not only to get the story out but also to avoid going to prison. By telling the truth, he might win immunity from prosecution—meaning that in return for his testimony against others, he would not be accused of crimes.

When Nixon learned that Dean was talking with the prosecutors, he summoned him to the White House. He wanted to get Dean to resign and also to see just how much Dean planned to tell the prosecutors.

The two met in the Oval Office the morning of April 16. Nixon said he would like to have Dean's resignation in hand, even though he did not plan to use it right away. Dean replied that he thought the president should also have the resignations of Haldeman and Ehrlichman handy, since they too had taken part in the cover-up. Nixon resisted.

"I thought Dean at this moment," the president said. He then handed Dean two papers to consider. One said:

> Dear Mr. President:
> As a result of my involvement in the Watergate matter, which we discussed last night and today, I tender to you my resignation effective at once.

The other said:

> Dear Mr. President:
> In view of my increasing involvement in the Watergate matter, my impending appearance before the grand jury and the probability of its action, I request an immediate and indefinite leave of absence from my position on your staff.

Nixon asked Dean to sign both statements. Fearing he was being set up as a scapegoat, Dean refused. "What I would like to do is draft up for you an alternative letter putting in both options and you can just put them in the file," Dean said. "Short and sweet."

Nixon agreed.

(Dean did draft a letter of resignation, but in it he said he was resigning along with Haldeman and Ehrlichman. This was not what the president wanted.)

Ten minutes after his meeting with Dean, Nixon called in Ehrlichman and Haldeman to tell them about the session. "This is one smooth operator," he said of Dean.

Later that afternoon Haldeman outlined a scenario in which Nixon would say publicly that Dean had just told him about the Watergate cover-up, that he had known nothing about it before, and that he was surprised to learn of Dean's involvement.

"Now look," Nixon replied, "I don't want to get into the position of . . ."

"Hanging someone else?" Haldeman replied. "Well, but he is going to have hung himself at that point in time."

Still, Nixon was cautious. He noted that Dean had knowledge about other matters. "See what I mean?" said Nixon. "I don't want him—he is in possession of knowledge about things that happened before this [such as the illegal wiretaps and the Ellsberg break-in]. I told him that was all national security."

Despite his qualms, Nixon ultimately did decide to make Dean the scapegoat.

The next day, Nixon publicly announced that "major developments" in the Watergate case had come to his attention and that he would allow his aides to testify in the case instead of continuing to claim executive privilege.

And, in a slap at Dean, he said, "No individual holding, in the past or at present, a position of major importance in the administration, should be given immunity from prosecution."

Dean, hoping to win immunity, took this as a sign of war. He went to his White House office, gathered up a bunch of papers on Watergate, and went home to prepare his story for the prosecutors.

Meanwhile, Magruder also was talking. He told the prosecutors that John Mitchell, the former attorney general and later head of the reelection committee, had approved the Watergate break-in. He also implicated John Dean and other White House and committee officials.

Magruder stopped by the White House to tell

Ehrlichman and Haldeman what he was doing. He found out later that they had taped the conversations to use in their own defense. The men who had planned burglaries, wiretaps, and other illegal activities were not ready to stand by one another when their misdeeds were discovered. It was every man for himself.

Toward the end of April, Nixon realized that he would have to get rid of Ehrlichman and Haldeman as well as Dean. But he was reluctant to do so, as he revealed in a conversation with Assistant Attorney General Henry E. Petersen, who was in charge of the initial investigation into Watergate by the Justice Department.

"I am not in communication with Dean at all, for obvious reasons," Nixon told Petersen, referring to Dean's decision to talk to the prosecutors. "But Haldeman and Ehrlichman, I hold my damn brain sessions [with them]. I know that they are telling me the truth. Dean, I can't believe him. Because I don't know what he is up to, you see? . . . I don't like to put the three of them in the same bag. Although they may all be there."

By this time, however, it was clear that both Haldeman and Ehrlichman would have to go. The details Dean was giving the prosecutors were leaking out daily. Both men would be called before the Watergate grand jury to testify and might be charged with criminal actions.

On April 30 Nixon announced the resignations of Haldeman and Ehrlichman—"two of the finest public servants it has been my privilege to know"—and the dismissal of John Dean. Attorney General Kleindienst resigned as well.

In the speech, Nixon talked about what Watergate was doing to the country.

> Some people, quite properly appalled at the abuses that occurred, will say that Watergate demonstrates the bankruptcy of the American political system.
>
> I believe precisely the opposite is true. Watergate represented a series of illegal acts and bad judg-

ments by a number of individuals. It was the system that has brought the facts to light and that will bring those guilty to justice—a system that in this case has included a determined grand jury, honest prosecutors, a courageous judge, John Sirica, and a vigorous free press.

Nixon was exactly right. The system *was* working to find the truth and punish the guilty. But he did not realize just how thorough a job the system would do.

9

THE INVESTIGATORS TAKE OVER

AFTER ATTORNEY GENERAL RICHARD KLEINDIENST RE-signed, Congress decided that an outsider was needed to take over the Watergate investigation. It no longer trusted the Justice Department to do the job because of the way the FBI and federal prosecutors had worked so cozily with the White House the first time around.

Nixon moved the top man at the Pentagon, Elliot L. Richardson, over to the Justice Department to replace Kleindienst. Richardson promised to appoint an outsider to the Watergate case.

The man he chose to head the independent investigation was Archibald Cox, a law professor at Harvard who had worked in Washington under two former Democratic presidents, Harry S. Truman and John F. Kennedy.

Cox had a reputation for fairness, and his appointment was praised by Democrats and Republicans alike as well as in newspaper editorials. Cox said he would try to "restore confidence in the honor, integrity and decency of government."

Cox had the title of special prosecutor. His job was to find out what laws had been broken in the Watergate case and to seek court convictions against the men who had acted illegally.

At the same time that Cox was starting to put a team of

investigators together, the Senate Watergate Committee was getting ready to open its hearings. Cox thought the hearings should be postponed so they would not interfere with the criminal cases he planned to develop. But Senator Sam Ervin (Dem., North Carolina), head of the Watergate Committee, rejected that idea. He knew it took a long time to get cases tried in court.

"The American people are entitled to find out what actually happened without having to wait while justice travels on leaden feet," Ervin said. Judge Sirica agreed and ruled that the hearings would go ahead as scheduled.

The Senate Watergate Committee had seven members. Besides Ervin, the chairman, there were three other Democrats—Herman Talmadge (Georgia), Daniel Inouye (Hawaii), and Joseph Montoya (New Mexico). Senator Howard H. Baker, Jr. (Tennessee), a Republican, was the vice chairman, and there were two other Republicans—Lowell Weicker (Connecticut) and Edward Gurney (Florida).

Sam Dash was the staff director and chief lawyer for the Democrats. Fred Thompson was the chief lawyer for the Republicans.

Although members of Congress often work at cross purposes for political reasons, the senators on the Watergate Committee managed to overcome this problem to a large degree. The two sides worked well together. Little by little the story of Watergate unfolded during the hearings. It was an amazing tale of robbery, intrigue, spying, evasion, and lies, all at the highest levels of the federal government under Richard Nixon.

As the hearings opened on May 17, 1973, Senator Ervin said, "The investigation of this select committee was born of crisis, unabated as of this very time, the crisis of a mounting loss of confidence of American citizens in the integrity of our electoral process." The purpose of the hearings was "to provide full and open public testimony in order that the nation can proceed toward the healing of the wounds that now afflict the body politic."

"The nation and history are watching us," Ervin said. "We cannot fail our mission."

Among the first witnesses at the Senate hearings was James McCord, the Watergate burglar who had helped break the story open. McCord was asked why, "after a lifetime of work as a law enforcement officer" with the CIA, he had agreed to go along with a series of burglaries and with illegal wiretaps on telephones.

"A very important reason to me was the fact that the attorney general himself, Mr. John Mitchell, had . . . considered and approved the operation, according to Mr. Liddy," McCord replied.

He added that Liddy had told him that John Dean also had taken part in the decision. With these two top government lawyers giving approval, McCord said, he figured there must be a good, patriotic reason for the wiretapping.

"I felt that the attorney general, in his position as the top legal officer, if this operation were clearly illegal, would turn it down out of hand."

McCord also described the paranoia that prevailed at the Nixon reelection committee in 1972. He said the committee had feared that the Democratic presidential candidate, George McGovern, had an undercover agent who was feeding him important GOP papers and that anti-Nixon groups were planning violent activities to disrupt the Republican national convention. He said the Republicans had wanted to find out if anyone on the staff of McGovern or Democratic National Chairman Larry O'Brien was secretly supporting the violent groups.

McCord testified that after the burglars were caught and it was clear that they would go to jail, Howard Hunt assured him that money would be forthcoming to take care of his family and that "the defendants were going to be provided with, given executive clemency [the president would order them freed], after a period of time in prison."

In addition, McCord said that during his January 1973 trial he met in secret several times with John Caulfield, a former policeman who had been hired by the White House to work on undercover projects. Sometimes he met with Caulfield directly, McCord said, and sometimes it was more mysterious.

> I received a call from an unidentified individ-
> ual who said that Caulfield was out of town and

asked me to go to a pay phone booth near the Blue
Fountain Inn on Route 355 near my residence,
where he had a message for me from Caulfield.
There the same individual called and read the following message:

"Plead guilty. One year is a long time. You will
get executive clemency. Your family will be taken
care of and when you get out you will be rehabili-
tated and a job will be found for you. Don't take
immunity when called before the grand jury."

McCord said he did not know who had made the call,
but he had several subsequent meetings with Caulfield, where
the message was repeated. McCord said that when he made it
clear that he did not plan to go along, Caulfield told him he
was "fouling up the game plan" and followed up with an indirect threat. "He responded by saying that, 'you know that if
the administration gets its back to the wall, it will have to take
steps to defend itself.' I took that as a personal threat."

Caulfield, who followed McCord on the witness stand,
confirmed most of what McCord had said but indicated that
he had not meant to threaten the Watergate burglar. Rather,
he was just giving him "a small piece of friendly advice."

Caulfield said he had made the offer of clemency—which
can be given only by the president—at the insistence of John
Dean. He said Dean had instructed him to tell McCord that
the offer came "from the very highest levels of the White
House."

"At the meeting with Mr. Dean, he also impressed upon
me that this was a very grave situation which might someday
threaten the president," Caulfield said, "that it had the potential of becoming a national scandal."

In response to Caulfield's testimony, President Nixon issued a statement saying he had never authorized anyone on
his staff to promise clemency to the burglars. Indeed, it appeared that members of the White House staff were promising
more than they could deliver in an effort to keep the burglars
quiet.

Caulfield revealed that McCord's mystery caller had been an old friend, Anthony Ulasewicz, a former colleague in the New York City Police Department. He said Ulasewicz had made the call as a favor to him because he was reluctant to get involved. But he talked with McCord himself later anyway because, he said, "I believed I was doing something for the president of the U.S."

Ulasewicz testified briefly as well, adding a light note to the proceedings by expressing amazement that a party of five men had been sent in to install wiretaps at the Watergate.

If the New York police were going to install a wiretap, he said, they "would not have walked in with any army, that is for sure."

The second Watergate burglar to testify was Bernard Barker. Barker's testimony revealed why the Miami men had taken part in the burglary—they trusted Howard Hunt and thought that if they helped him in an undercover operation, he would help them.

Their goal, Barker said, was to win U.S. support to overthrow the Communist dictator in Cuba, Fidel Castro.

"E. Howard Hunt, under the name of Eduardo, represents to the Cuban people their liberation," Barker said, adding that he had worked with Hunt in the early 1960s in the Bay of Pigs Invasion against Castro. "Eduardo represents the liberation of Cuba."

Thus, early in the hearings the motives of the Watergate burglars themselves became clear. The Miami men had blindly followed Howard Hunt in the belief that he would help them free Cuba from the Communists. And McCord had been conditioned by years in the CIA to follow orders without asking too many searching questions.

When Jeb Magruder, the former number-two man on the Nixon reelection committee, appeared before the Senate panel, he was asked how he had come to the decision that breaking into offices was acceptable.

Magruder responded with a story about a course he had taken in ethics at Yale University from a respected professor, William Sloane Coffin. Magruder noted that Coffin was active in the movement against the Vietnam War and had urged

young men to burn their draft cards and try to shut down
Washington with mass demonstrations.

"Now here are ethical, legitimate people whom I respected," Magruder said. "I respect Mr. Coffin tremen-
dously. . . . I saw people I was very close to breaking the law
without any regard for any other person's pattern of behavior
or belief. So consequently, when these subjects came up, although I was aware they were illegal, we had become some-
what inured [accustomed to the idea]."

Magruder also was asked why, after the burglars were
caught, the committee did not just admit what had happened
and take the consequences.

"I do not think there was ever any discussion that there
would not be a cover-up," he said. "I think it was felt that if it
ever reached Mr. Mitchell [the Nixon campaign chairman] before the election, the president would lose the election."

Day by day the story of Watergate unfolded. Television
cameras carried the testimony into homes all across the nation,
and as the weeks wore on, the TV audience grew. In homes, in
offices, everywhere, people were talking about Watergate, who
to believe, and where the story might lead.

Meanwhile, behind the scenes, Sam Dash, chief in-
vestigator for the Senate committee, was secretly talking with
John Dean. Dash wanted Dean to tell his story in full, and the
two men spent days together going over the details, point by
point.

But Dean would not testify unless he was promised immunity—that is, he did not want anything he said in the hearings to be used against him in court. After Dash heard what
Dean had to say, he felt that all Americans should hear it. So
he asked Judge Sirica to grant Dean's request.

Sirica did grant Dean immunity, but it was of a limited
kind. While nothing Dean said in the Senate hearings would
be used against him, that did not mean that he could not be
indicted by a grand jury if prosecutors found other evidence
against him (which they did).

Dean agreed to these terms and began putting together
his story. It would be a blockbuster.

10

JOHN DEAN'S SENATE TESTIMONY

THE TALE THAT JOHN DEAN TOLD AT THE SENATE WATER-gate hearings was high drama. Millions of Americans stayed glued to their television sets for the entire week he was in the witness chair. Some cheered him on, while many others saw him as a whiny traitor, a man trying to bring down the president to save his own skin.

Dean said that when he joined the White House as a young lawyer in July 1970, he was surprised at the "strong feelings that the president and his staff had toward antiwar demonstrators—and demonstrators in general." He claimed that "the White House was continually seeking intelligence information about demonstration leaders and their supporters that would either discredit them personally or indicate that the demonstration was in fact sponsored by some foreign enemy."

Suspicion also ran high that political leaders who opposed the war were tied to the demonstrations. Although no proof was ever found to support any of these beliefs, Dean said, the president continued to think there was a plot against him. Nixon blamed the lack of evidence on a lack of good undercover work among his own forces.

"We never found . . . evidence indicating that these demonstrators were part of a master plan; nor that they were funded by the Democratic political funds; nor that they had any direct connection with the McGovern campaign," Dean said. "This was explained to Mr. Haldeman, but the president believed that the opposite was, in fact, true."

In this atmosphere, Dean said, the White House ordered wiretaps on the telephones of reporters and others and considered some alarmingly bizarre plans.

For example, Dean said, a man who had worked on the White House National Security Council—and thus had access to government secrets—later went to work at a Washington research agency called the Brookings Institution.

When the White House learned that Brookings was planning to publish a study on Vietnam "based on documents of a current nature," it feared that the former White House worker had taken classified information with him when he took the job at Brookings.

Dean said that Nixon aide Charles Colson proposed firebombing the Brookings Institution. It would create a lot of confusion, he reasoned, and give a White House undercover agent the opportunity to slip inside and look for the secret papers.

Fortunately, Dean said, Colson asked John Caulfield (the former New York City policeman) to do the job, and Caulfield was appalled. He appealed to Dean to kill the idea. "What prompted Mr. Caulfield to come to me was that he thought the matter was most unwise and that his instructions from Colson were insane," said Dean. "I arranged to see Ehrlichman and told him that the burglary of Brookings was insane and probably impossible. He said OK and he called Mr. Colson off of it."

Dean said that the White House also was determined to dig up dirt on Senator Edward Kennedy because the president and his men considered him a political threat.

Kennedy had gotten in trouble in 1969 when he drove off a bridge at Chappaquiddick, Massachusetts, after a party and a young woman in the car with him drowned. Dean said that the White House tried for years to find out other damaging information about Kennedy and in 1971 proposed putting him under surveillance (having someone watch him all the time).

The surveillance idea came to Dean from Lawrence

Higby, Bob Haldeman's top aide. "After some initial re-
sistance, I convinced Higby that it was a bad idea and the day-
in, day-out surveillance concept was called off," Dean said,
although the White House continued to pay close attention to
everything Kennedy did.

"In addition to the extensive efforts to obtain politically
embarrassing information on Senator Kennedy, there were also
frequent efforts to obtain politically embarrassing information
on Mr. Lawrence O'Brien, the Democratic National Committee chairman, Senator Muskie and Senator McGovern [both
potential presidential candidates]," Dean said.

The White House interest in digging up dirt on Democrats put a lot of pressure on the Nixon reelection committee.
John Mitchell and Jeb Magruder were told to get more, more,
more.

According to Dean, when the committee began looking
around for someone to do undercover work, the name of G.
Gordon Liddy came up. He was recommended to Dean by
Egil Krogh, an Ehrlichman aide. "Krogh spoke very highly of
Liddy's ability as a lawyer and said that his FBI–Treasury Department background in law enforcement would qualify him to
handle a demonstration, intelligence and security operation for
the re-election committee," Dean said.

So Liddy was hired and told to come up with a plan for
getting better information on the president's opponents. Dean
went on to describe the proposal that Liddy presented to him,
Mitchell, and Magruder in a meeting on January 27, 1972.

> I did not fully understand everything Mr.
> Liddy was recommending at the time because some
> of the concepts were mind-boggling. Plans called for
> mugging squads, kidnapping teams, prostitutes to
> compromise the opposition, and electronic sur-
> veillance. He explained that the mugging squad
> could, for example, rough up demonstrators that
> were causing problems. The kidnapping teams
> could remove demonstration leaders and take them
> below the Mexican border.

While these ideas were rejected, Dean said, Liddy was back a week later with a revised plan that focused more on wiretaps. No decision was made in that meeting. But four months later Dean learned of the Liddy-led break-in at the Democratic National Committee headquarters in the Watergate.

Dean said that in the days immediately following the break-in he met or talked with most top White House and reelection committee aides about the problem. The idea was to make sure that no one found out it was linked to the White House.

He also met with Liddy. "Liddy was very apologetic for the fact that they had been caught and that Mr. McCord was involved," Dean said, since McCord worked directly for the reelection committee. "He told me that he had used Mr. McCord only because Magruder had cut his budget so badly. He also told me that he was a soldier and would never talk. He said that if anyone wished to shoot him on the street, he was ready."

Others were far more practical, said Dean:

• Gordon Strachan, a top aide to Haldeman, "told me that he had been instructed by Haldeman to go through all of Mr. Haldeman's files over the weekend [after the break-in] and remove and destroy damaging materials," including anything on wiretaps or spying on McGovern or Muskie.

• White House officials opened the safe that Howard Hunt kept in his office in the White House. They found all kinds of information that could have caused them trouble—information about the break-in at Daniel Ellsberg's psychiatrist's office in the Pentagon Papers case, papers aimed at making Senator Kennedy look bad, and an assessment of the Plumbers unit, which had been involved in wiretaps to plug leaks of information.

Dean said that Ehrlichman "told me to shred the documents and deep six the briefcase. I asked him what he meant by 'deep six.' He leaned back in his chair and said: 'you drive across the river on your

way home at night don't you?' I said yes. He said, 'Well, when you cross over the bridge on your way home, just toss the briefcase into the river.'" Dean did not follow Ehrlichman's instructions. Instead he gave the material to Patrick Gray, who burned it.
• The White House tried to convince the CIA to give money to the Watergate burglars, but the CIA resisted. Deputy Director Vernon Walters told Dean that "the director would only do it on a direct order from the president." The White House dropped the idea.
• On September 12, just weeks before the 1972 presidential election, Dean had a conversation with Nixon about the break-in and its aftermath. Dean said that Nixon expressed hope that the Watergate burglars would not be tried until after the election. "The conversation then moved to the press coverage of the Watergate incident and how the press was really trying to make this into a major campaign issue," Dean said. "At one point in this conversation, I recall the president telling me to keep a good list of the press people giving us trouble, because we will make life difficult for them after the election." (Five months after the election the *Washington Post*, the newspaper that had the most aggressive coverage of Watergate in 1972, won a Pulitzer Prize for its efforts.)

Dean said that Nixon also stressed how he wanted to use the Internal Revenue Service to harass his enemies. The IRS collects taxes, and all of the information it receives is confidential. It is against the law for the IRS to give someone's personal tax information to the president or anyone else—as Nixon well knew.

Dean also outlined his later meetings with Nixon, describing how much Nixon appeared to know about the cover-up, his discussion of payoffs for the burglars and possible clemency for them, and his desire that the story be kept secret.

Among Dean's most shocking revelations was the existence of a White House "enemies list." This was simply a long list of names of people that the White House considered enemies—politicians, labor leaders, business leaders, reporters, editors, professors, and movie stars.

Dean gave the Senate committee a copy of the list, along with a memo he had written in 1971 titled "dealing with our political enemies." In the memo, Dean outlined "how we can use the available federal machinery to screw our political enemies."

The list was a sensation. By now the Nixon administration had become so unpopular that there was no shame in being disliked by it. In fact, many of those on the "enemies list" joked that it was a distinct honor.

Dean spent an entire day reading a 245-page account of Watergate that he had written beforehand. The rest of the week he answered questions. Several members of the committee, especially those who strongly supported the president, were skeptical of his story.

"Mr. Dean, you realize of course that you have made very strong charges against the president of the United States that involves him in criminal offenses, do you not?" asked Senator Talmadge. "What makes you think that your credibility is greater than that of the president, who denies what you have said?"

"I have told it exactly the way I know it," Dean replied.

When Senator Baker questioned Dean, he came up with a catchy phrase that eventually became the key question of Watergate: "What did the president know, and when did he know it?"

Baker asked Dean if Nixon knew about the Watergate break-in before it occurred. Dean said, "I do not know for a fact" that he did.

Baker then asked what—and when—Nixon knew about the cover-up. Dean said that when he met with Nixon on September 15, 1972, it was clear that Nixon knew about the cover-up. But Dean made it clear that both Haldeman and Ehrlichman, who met with Nixon regularly on important matters, knew much earlier and most likely had discussed Water-gate and its aftermath with the president.

Jeb Magruder had, like Dean, agreed to tell his story to the prosecutors in hopes of getting a lighter punishment. He testi-fied that Mitchell was the one who had approved Liddy's plan for the Watergate break-in. The decision, Magruder said, was made on March 30 at a meeting in Key Biscayne, Florida. He said that he, Mitchell, and a close aide, Fred LaRue, were the only ones present.

MAGRUDER: As I recall it was the last item brought up at our meeting. It had the figures and the amounts and it was quite obvious what they were for . . . and we discussed the pros and cons, Mr. LaRue and Mr. Mitchell and I. . . . Mr. Mitchell simply signed off on it in the sense of saying, "Okay, let's give him a quarter of a million dol-lars and let's see what he can come up with."
BAKER: You say Mr. Mitchell simply signed off on it. Do you mean physically initialed it or signed it?
MAGRUDER: No sir, I mean said, we will give Mr. Liddy the $250,000.
BAKER: And he identified the targets? Did that include the Demo-cratic National Committee headquarters at the Watergate?
MAGRUDER: Yes, sir.
BAKER: Was there any question in your mind that the plan was agreed to by Mr. Mitchell?
MAGRUDER: No sir, there was no doubt. But it was a reluctant deci-sion. I think it is important to note. It was not one that anyone was overwhelmed with at all. But it was made and he did make it.
BAKER: Tell me more about why it was a reluctant decision.
MAGRUDER: We knew it was illegal, probably inappropriate. We didn't think that much would come of it.

Mitchell's testimony before the committee told a different story. He was questioned by the Democratic majority's chief counsel, Dash.

DASH: Now, what is your recollection of what decision you made in Key Biscayne on the so-called Liddy plan?
MITCHELL: Well, it was very simple. [It was] "This again, we don't

need this. I am tired of hearing it. Out. Let's not discuss it any further. This sort of a concept."

DASH: Then how do you explain, Mr. Mitchell, Mr. Magruder's sworn testimony that you, however reluctantly, approved the quarter million dollar Liddy plan at Key Biscayne?

MITCHELL: Mr. Dash, I can't explain anybody's testimony up here but my own.

When John Ehrlichman got to the witness stand, he also denied having done anything wrong. "I am here to refute every charge of illegal conduct on my part which has been made during the course of these hearings," he said. "Let's be clear: I did not cover up anything to do with Watergate." Ehrlichman was asked many questions about the Watergate affair, but he continued to insist that he had not been involved.

He also said something that stunned the senators. It related not to the Watergate break-in but to an earlier crime—the break-in at a psychiatrist's office by Liddy and Hunt, who were looking for the psychiatrist's evaluation of Daniel Ellsberg. Ehrlichman said he thought the break-in was perfectly legal: "I considered the special unit's [the Plumbers'] activities to be well within the president's inherent constitutional powers, and this particular episode, the break-in in California, likewise to have been within the president's inherent constitutional powers. . . ." The reason, Ehrlichman said, was that the president can do almost anything "to prevent the betrayal of national security secrets."

Ehrlichman added that he had not personally authorized the break-in at Ellsberg's psychiatrist's office. But he did not see anything wrong with it, either.

Bob Haldeman's testimony was equally interesting. Although he had a reputation as the man in the White House who kept a finger on everything, he portrayed himself differently. Haldeman said he had not been very involved with the president's reelection committee in 1972 or with the campaign's tangled finances—and certainly not with plans leading up to the Watergate break-in or the cover-up that followed.

"Dean moved in immediately after the incident as sort of the Watergate project officer in the White House," Haldeman said. "This was in keeping with our usual procedure; the responsibility was his and he had the authority to proceed. Dean kept Ehrlichman and me posted from time to time on developments, and, through us, the president. He apparently did not keep us fully posted and it now appears he did not keep us accurately posted."

At the time, Haldeman said, he and the president and Ehrlichman were so busy with more important matters that they paid scant attention to the Watergate case. "The view of all three of us through the whole period was that the truth must be told, and quickly; although we didn't know what the truth was," Haldeman said. "Every time we pushed for action in this direction we were told by Dean that it could not be done . . . as it now appears, we were badly misled by one or more of the principals and even more so by our own man, for reasons which are still not completely clear."

Haldeman added, "At no time did I give Dean any instructions to cover up anything in this case. . . . I had no personal motivation to cover up anything because I had no personal involvement and I knew the president had no involvement."

Who would the Senate committee—and the public—believe? Dean, or Haldeman and Ehrlichman? Magruder, or Mitchell?

A Gallup public opinion poll taken a couple of weeks after the Senate Watergate Committee recessed on August 7 found that America's opinion was divided. Fifty-two percent of those polled thought the hearings had been good for the country, while 41 percent thought they were bad for the country. Fifty-seven percent thought the Watergate Committee was more interested in getting the facts about Watergate than in trying to discredit President Nixon; 28 percent thought the opposite.

For many people, these doubts would linger throughout 1973 and into 1974. But a battle loomed ahead that would ultimately skew opinion heavily in Dean's favor.

G. Gordon Liddy, who dreamed up the break-in at the Watergate after crazier plans he had submitted were rejected by the president's reelection committee. After the burglars were caught Liddy told White House lawyer John Dean, "This is my fault and I'm prepared to accept responsibility for it. And if somebody wants to shoot me on a street corner, I'm prepared to have that done."

(Copyright © Washington Post; reprinted by permission of the D.C. Public Library)

E. Howard Hunt, Jr.,
a longtime
undercover agent for
the Central
Intelligence Agency
who helped direct the
Watergate burglary.
He put heavy
pressure on the
White House for
"hush money" after
he was arrested. Hunt
wrote spy thrillers
when he wasn't
skulking around the
dark side himself.
*(Copyright © Washington
Post; reprinted by
permission of the D.C.
Public Library)*

James W. McCord, Jr., was the first of the
Watergate burglars to break the code of
silence all had honored since their arrest.
He was infuriated to see reelection
committee officials who helped plan the
burglary going to parties while he was
headed for jail.

Jeb Stuart Magruder was number-two man at the Nixon reelection committee and one of those who sat in on the meetings where the Watergate burglary and other dirty deeds were planned. When the burglars were arrested, the first person that Gordon Liddy called was Jeb Magruder.

(Copyright © Washington Post; reprinted by permission of the D.C. Public Library)

John Dean was a cocky young lawyer when he joined the White House team, thrilled to be so close to the center of power and the president of the United States. But as Watergate problems engulfed him, he grew disillusioned and depressed. His testimony before the Senate Watergate Committee electrified the nation and infuriated Richard Nixon.

(Copyright © Washington Post; reprinted by permission of the D.C. Public Library)

John N. Mitchell was a rich and distinguished lawyer when he met Richard Nixon. By the time the Watergate trials were over, he was a broken man.

(Copyright © Washington Post; reprinted by permission of the D.C. Public Library)

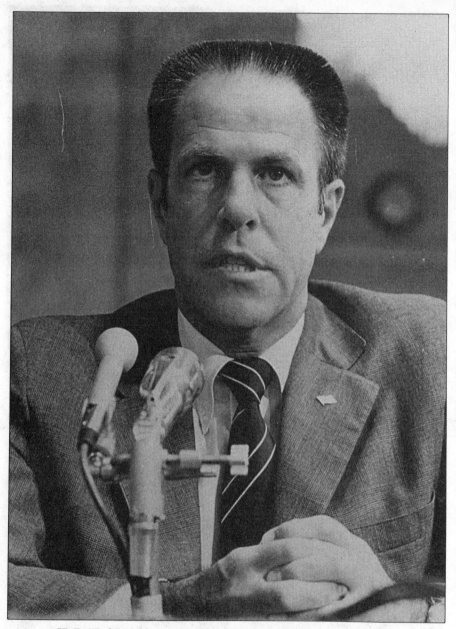

H. R. "Bob" Haldeman was President Nixon's chief of staff and part of what Nixon called his "brain trust." A reprimand from Haldeman brought chills to lower-ranking men in the White House. He was cold and demanding, the president's henchman.

John D. Ehrlichman was the third most powerful man at the White House after Nixon and Haldeman. He told John Dean to throw a briefcase full of incriminating papers into the Potomac River. Dean didn't take the suggestion.

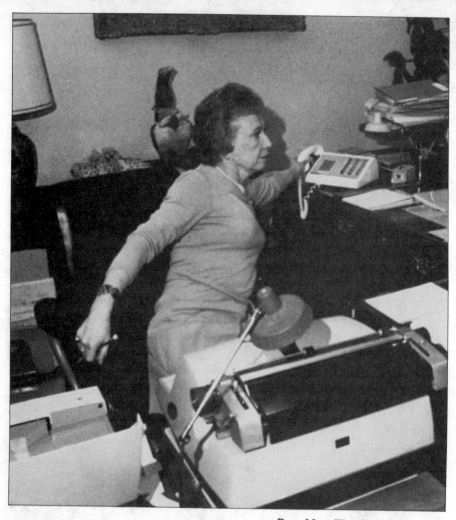

Rose Mary Woods, President Nixon's personal secretary, testified in court that she had no idea how eighteen minutes of the tape of the June 20, 1972, meeting between President Nixon and Haldeman were erased.

(UPI/Bettmann Newsphotos)

L. Patrick Gray, Jr., was the acting FBI director who went along with White House efforts to limit the initial investigation into Watergate. He burned evidence related to Watergate that the White House asked him to destroy, setting it ablaze along with the Christmas trash.

(Copyright © Washington Post; reprinted by permission of the D.C. Public Library)

Archibald Cox, independent prosecutor
who delved into the secrets of Watergate
with great energy and imagination.
President Nixon ordered him fired in the
"Saturday Night Massacre."

*(Copyright © Washington Post; reprinted by
permission of the D.C. Public Library)*

Senator Howard Baker
asked the key question in
the Watergate hearings:
"What did the president
know, and when did he
know it?"

*(Copyright © Washington Post;
reprinted by permission of the
D.C. Public Library)*

Senator Baker with Senator Sam Ervin, the folksy and widely respected chairman of the Senate Watergate Committee.

The Senate Watergate hearings in session. H. R. Haldeman is in the witness chair, denying any involvement in the burglary or the cover-up.

President Nixon bids farewell to the White House staff after his resignation. His wife Pat, is right ahead of him. Behind him on the podium are his daughter Tricia and her husband, Edward Cox.

(Copyright © Washington Post; reprinted by permission of the D.C. Public Library)

President Nixon says an emotional farewell to members of his cabinet and staff in the White House before leaving for California. Behind him are his wife Pat and his daughters Julie and Tricia and their husbands David Eisenhower and Edward Cox.

(UPI/Bettmann Newsphotos)

President Nixon and Pat say
good-bye to the new president,
Gerald Ford, and his wife
Betty.

*(Copyright © Washington Post;
reprinted by permission of the D.C.
Public Library)*

President Nixon waves with both arms as he boards
a helicopter on the South Lawn of the White House
for the first part of a flight to California after an
emotional farewell to members of his staff.
(UPI)

11

THE FIGHT FOR
THE WHITE HOUSE
TAPES

ALEXANDER P. BUTTERFIELD, AN OBSCURE WHITE HOUSE OF-
ficial, electrified the Senate Watergate hearings when he
testified on July 16, 1973. He revealed to the American public
for the first time that conversations in the Oval Office had
been tape-recorded since 1970.

Butterfield said that in his job as deputy assistant to the
president, he made sure that the White House ran smoothly
and that important presidential material was preserved for history. One of his tasks was to see that the tape-recording system
operated properly. The idea, Butterfield said, was to have President Nixon's conversations available for historians in the future.

Fred Thompson (chief Republican lawyer for the Senate
committee) led Butterfield into the revelation.

THOMPSON: Mr. Butterfield, are you aware of the installation of any
listening devices in the Oval Office of the president?
BUTTERFIELD: I was aware of listening devices, yes sir.
THOMPSON: When were those devices placed in the Oval Office?
BUTTERFIELD: Approximately the summer of 1970.
THOMPSON: Are you aware of any devices that were installed in the
Executive Office Building Office of the President?
BUTTERFIELD: Yes, sir, at that time.

THOMPSON: Were they installed at the same time?
BUTTERFIELD: They were installed at the same time.
THOMPSON: Would you tell us a little bit about how those devices worked, how they were activated, for example.
BUTTERFIELD: They were installed, of course, for historical purposes, to record the president's business, and they were installed in his two offices. . . .

Butterfield went on to explain that he and other White House officials kept track of where the president was in the White House offices through something called a "locator box." It had several lights on top, and whenever the president moved from one location to another in the White House, officials would push one of the buttons to indicate where the president was. When a light atop the locator box went on, the taping system in the room indicated by the light would be turned on. When someone in the room began to talk, the tape started to roll. In this way, all of the president's conversations in the White House would be preserved for history.

"There is no doubt in my mind that they were installed to record things for posterity, for the Nixon library," Butterfield said, referring to a library that would hold papers from the Nixon presidency after he left office. "The president was very conscious of that kind of thing. We had quite an elaborate set-up at the White House for the collection and preservation of documents and of things which transpired in the way of business of state."

Butterfield said that the tape recorders had been installed at Nixon's direction and that only a few other people knew they were in operation—Haldeman, Haldeman's assistant Lawrence Higby, and some members of the Secret Service. He explained that the tapes were checked each day and carefully stored away without being transcribed.

The fact that Nixon had bugged his own offices shocked those at the hearing and the millions of Americans watching the proceedings on television. The idea that there could be a record—an indisputable record—of the president's conversations was, to most people, unsettling.

It meant that everything that was said in private between

Nixon and his aides—or foreign leaders, or governors, or members of Congress—had been recorded on a tape. Surveys taken shortly after Butterfield's testimony showed that three out of four Americans disapproved of the secret taping. They were repelled by the idea of bugging the Oval Office.

But the fact that the tapes had been made meant there was proof of what had gone on in the secret counsels of the White House during the months following the Watergate break-in.

Sam Dash pointed out just how significant this revelation was when he questioned Butterfield.

DASH: The tapes you mentioned were stored; are they stored by a particular date?

BUTTERFIELD: Yes, sir.

DASH: And so that if either Mr. Dean, Mr. Haldeman, Mr. Ehrlichman or Mr. Colson had particular meetings in the Oval Office with the president on any particular dates that have been testified before this committee, there would be a tape recording with the president of that full conversation, would there not?

BUTTERFIELD: Yes, sir.

DASH: Just one last question. If one were therefore to reconstruct the conversations at any particular date, what would be the best way to reconstruct those conversations, Mr. Butterfield, in the president's Oval Office?

BUTTERFIELD: Well, in the obvious manner, Mr. Dash—to obtain the tape and play it.

Obtain the tape and play it! That would show who was telling the truth, Richard Nixon and his still-loyal aides, or John Dean. It seemed simple enough. The tapes would reveal the truth.

With that in mind, the Senate Watergate Committee immediately asked the White House for tapes made on the days when key conversations about Watergate had taken place. Special prosecutor Archibald Cox made the same request.

Nixon refused both requests. The battle lines were drawn. The president would not give up the tapes. The Senate

Committee and the special prosecutor were determined to have them.

The committee then issued a subpoena—a legal order—demanding the tapes. Also, Judge John Sirica signed a subpoena for the tapes at the request of Archibald Cox to use in his criminal investigation of Watergate.

Nixon continued to refuse to hand over the tapes, despite the subpoenas. He argued that neither the judicial branch (Sirica) nor the legislative branch (Congress) could tell the executive branch (Nixon) what to do. His legal argument was that the separation of powers inherent in the U.S. Constitution prevented him from having to obey such a subpoena.

Nixon also took his case to the public. In a nationally televised statement on August 15, 1973, he argued that releasing the tapes would set a horrible precedent and make it harder for future presidents to do their job.

A much more important principle is involved in this question than what the tapes might prove about Watergate. Each day a president of the United States is required to make difficult decisions on grave issues. It is absolutely necessary, if the president is to be able to do his job as the country expects, that he be able to talk openly and candidly with his advisers about issues and individuals.

The same kind of privacy is needed in conversations with other government officials and foreign leaders, Nixon said.

If I were to make public these tapes, containing as they do blunt and candid remarks on many different subjects, the confidentiality of the office of the president would always be suspect from now on. It would make no difference whether it was to serve the interests of a court, of a Senate committee or the president himself—the same damage would be done to the principle, and that damage would be irreparable. Persons talking with the president would never again be sure that recordings or notes of what they said would not suddenly be made public.

No one would want to advance tentative ideas that might later seem unsound. No diplomat would want to speak candidly in those sensitive negotiations which could bring peace or avoid war. No senator or congressman would want to talk frankly about the congressional horse-trading that might get a vital bill passed. No one would want to speak bluntly about public figures, here and abroad.

That is why I shall continue to oppose efforts which would set a precedent that would cripple all future presidents by inhibiting conversations between them and those they look to for advice.

The principle of confidentiality of presidential conversations is at stake in the question of these tapes.

A week later, at a news conference, Nixon noted that the elaborate White House taping system had been dismantled after Butterfield's revelations. "I'm just as happy that we don't [have it any longer]," he said.

But by refusing to turn over the tapes in response to the court subpoena, President Nixon put himself on a collision course with the judicial branch of the government. The situation worried legal scholars and ordinary citizens as well—in a democracy with three equal branches of government, what happens when a president refuses to obey a court order?

Judge Sirica was extremely worried about the standoff. When Nixon refused to obey the subpoena, special prosecutor Cox asked the judge to issue another order to enforce the subpoena. That would require the president to either turn over the tapes or give a good reason, "show cause," for failing to obey the court order.

Sirica signed the order and told both Cox and Nixon's lawyers to prepare their legal arguments on the issue. But as he later revealed in his book *To Set the Record Straight,* he was not happy about taking on the president of the United States.

> By signing the show cause order, I had for the first time in our history begun a real test of the limits of a president's so-called "executive privilege." Other presidents had invoked the privilege, but no president had ever been challenged in court on its use. . . . Here I was, an obscure judge, facing the president of the United States. The country was in a turmoil over the Watergate case. The president himself had been accused of illegal acts by his former counsel John Dean. Nixon had refused to turn over his tape recordings. He was obviously going to fight this scandal every step of the way, and had spent a lifetime fighting. I was approaching the most momentous decision of my life, and it made me extremely nervous. (pp. 106–107, Signet paperback edition)

Nixon hired a special lawyer to argue for him in court— Charles Alan Wright, a professor at the University of Texas law school and a specialist in constitutional law. Arguing against the president was special prosecutor Cox, also a constitutional scholar.

Both lawyers turned in thick packets of written arguments to Judge Sirica, which he studied before scheduling oral arguments in court on August 22, 1973. The large courtroom was crowded for the occasion. Nothing like this had ever occurred before, and people were anxious to see the battle between the two branches of government firsthand.

Wright spoke first. He argued, as Nixon had, that if the courts undermined the president's right to privacy, he would not be able to govern effectively.

Wright also emphasized that there was no precedent in American history of a court forcing a president to obey a subpoena. If Sirica tried to force Nixon to give up the tapes, he would be stepping into new legal territory—something judges do not like to do.

> No court has ever attempted to enforce a sub-poena directed at the president of the United States. No president—and for that matter no department head—has ever been held in contempt for refusing to produce information, either to the courts or to Congress, that the president has determined must be withheld in the public interest. . . .
>
> We must leave it to the good judgment of the president of the United States to determine whether the public interest permits disclosure of his most intimate documents. If we have doubts about the good judgment of any president, there are other forums in which those doubts are to be resolved, not in the United States District Court.

Cox agreed that there was no historical precedent to guide the judge—no court had ever enforced a subpoena against a president. But he said in his written argument that in the United States, no one—not even the president—is above the law.

> There is no exception for the president from the guiding principle that the public, in the pursuit of justice, has a right to every man's evidence. . . . Even the highest executive officials are subject to the rule of law, which it is emphatically the province and the duty of the courts to declare.

In Nixon's case, Cox argued in court,

> [T]here is strong reason to believe that the integrity of the executive offices has been corrupted,

although the extent of the rot is not yet clear. Confidence in our institutions is at stake.

Sirica's decision a week later came out as a kind of compromise. The judge ordered President Nixon to turn over the tapes, but not to the public. Instead, Sirica himself would examine the tapes privately. That way, the judge said, the president's privacy would be protected. The special prosecutor would get the information he needed to sort out who was telling the truth about conversations in the Oval Office, but nothing that would jeopardize national security.

The White House announced the following day that it would not comply with Sirica's order. The president decided to take the issue to a higher court, the U.S. Court of Appeals for the District of Columbia.

Because the case was so important, judges on the Appeals Court put all of their other business aside so they could hear the arguments right away. Attorneys Wright and Cox appeared before the Appeals Court on September 11. The judges conferred and two days later asked the two sides to try to reach a settlement out of court. Clearly, the Appeals Court was no more eager than Sirica had been to force the president's hand when there was no legal precedent for such an action.

Cox and the White House attorneys agreed. They met for three days, but in the end they failed to reach a compromise. The issue returned to the U.S. Court of Appeals. On October 12 the judges issued their opinion—they upheld Sirica's order. Nixon would have to turn the tapes over to the U.S. District Court judge.

At that point, most people expected Nixon to appeal to the U.S. Supreme Court. They thought there would be a standoff between the nation's highest court and the nation's top executive.

But that is not what happened.

12

THE SATURDAY NIGHT MASSACRE

INSTEAD OF ASKING THE SUPREME COURT FOR PERMISSION to keep the White House tapes secret, President Nixon proposed a compromise. The White House would listen to the tapes and make a summary of them, he said, and give that summary to special prosecutor Archibald Cox and to the Senate Watergate Committee. In return, Nixon said, the special prosecutor would have to agree not to subpoena any more tapes or other presidential papers.

Nixon knew that his critics would not be satisfied with a summary drawn up by the White House, so he said he would allow one outsider—Senator John C. Stennis, a Democrat from Mississippi—to listen to the tapes as well. That way, the president said, Stennis could verify that the summary released by the White House was accurate.

Before Nixon publicly announced this plan on October 19, 1973, he talked privately with everyone involved. He got general agreement from Senators Ervin and Baker, the men who headed the Senate Watergate Committee, and from Attorney General Elliot Richardson. Cox disagreed, but Nixon said that as Cox's ultimate boss he would direct him to go along with the plan anyway.

"Though I have not wished to intrude upon the independence of the special prosecutor," he said, "I have felt it necessary to direct him, as an employee of the executive branch, to make no further attempts by judicial process to obtain tapes, notes or memoranda of presidential conversations."

But Cox was not one to give up easily. At a news conference the day after Nixon's announcement, Cox outlined his reasons for refusing to comply. He noted that he was conducting a criminal investigation of White House officials, meaning that they could be found guilty of breaking the law and sent to prison.

In that situation, it was "simply not enough to make a compromise in which the real evidence is available only to two or three men operating in secrecy, all but one of them aides to the president." In addition, Cox said, while he might find information in the summaries that would lead to indictments of former White House officials, he would not be able to use the summaries themselves as evidence during a trial.

And finally, he said, he could not be sure that the White House would include in the summary all of the information he was seeking.

"I am not looking for a confrontation," he said, "[and] I'm certainly not out to get the president of the United States." But he refused to give up on getting the White House tapes.

Cox announced his refusal to go along with Nixon's plan on a Saturday morning. His reaction set off an amazing chain of events.

On Saturday afternoon Nixon ordered Attorney General Richardson to fire Cox for refusing to accept the compromise plan on the tapes.

Richardson, as the number-one man at the Justice Department and a member of the cabinet, could not refuse a direct order from the president. However, he disagreed with Nixon's decision to fire Cox, so he resigned himself.

The White House then turned to the number-two man at the Justice Department, Deputy Attorney General William D. Ruckelshaus, and ordered him to fire Cox. But Ruckelshaus also declined to go along with the president's decision. This infuriated the president. He fired Ruckelshaus.

Finally the White House turned to the Justice Department's number-three man, Solicitor Robert H. Bork. Bork agreed to carry out the president's order. He fired Cox.

The White House then announced that it was abolishing the special prosecutor's office altogether and transferring the Watergate investigation back to the Justice Department. That night FBI agents surrounded the offices Cox and his staff had been using and sealed them off so that no one could remove any files.

Americans were stunned by this fast-moving series of events. In homes, in restaurants, at golf courses and bowling alleys—everywhere people congregate all across the nation— the word spread quickly: "Did you hear? The president has fired the special prosecutor."

Surprise turned quickly to outrage. More than 350,000 people sent telegrams to Congress and the White House. Most were full of anger. They did not like what Nixon had done. Many wanted Congress to impeach him—to force him to leave office.

The firing of Cox and Ruckelshaus and the resignation of Richardson all occurred late on a Saturday. Thus, this devastating move by the White House came to be called the Saturday Night Massacre.

It was a turning point in the painful saga of Watergate. People who had supported the president previously now began to have doubts. And Nixon's critics said it showed that he did not want an honest investigation—that this proved he had a lot to cover up.

In the House of Representatives, Democrats introduced a flood of resolutions calling for impeachment of the president. A Republican, Representative Dan Kuykendall (Tennessee), accused his colleagues of acting like a lynch mob and held up a noose to show what he meant. Hisses started in the aisles of Congress and in the gallery where the public sat. The mood, both in Congress and among the public, was overwhelmingly against Richard Nixon.

Legislation also was introduced to require the president to appoint a new special prosecutor. This proposal was supported by Republicans as well as Democrats.

Nixon and his aides were caught off-guard by the ferocity of the reaction against his decision to fire Cox. The president had gambled that Americans would rally around him and turn on Cox. When they did not, the White House quickly changed course.

The following Tuesday, a hearing was scheduled before Judge Sirica because the court order requiring Nixon to turn over the tapes was still in effect.

The courtroom was full. The young lawyers who had been working with Archibald Cox were there despite Nixon's announcement that the office of the special prosecutor had been abolished. And the judge told the citizens serving on the grand jury investigating Watergate that their job was not done; even though Cox had been fired, the probe would continue.

So the air was filled with expectation when Charles Wright (the White House lawyer) approached the bench that Tuesday. Judge Sirica was so nervous that he misspoke. He read aloud an order he had written demanding that the president hand over the tapes. Then he said, "The court will now read the order," which he had just done.

Sirica was expecting continued defiance. To his surprise, however, attorney Wright announced that the president had changed his mind—he was now willing to hand over the tapes that Cox had requested, with the understanding that they would be heard in private by the judge.

Wright explained that Nixon had hoped his compromise plan—offering a summary of the tapes prepared by the White House—would "end a constitutional crisis." But, he added,

> The events of the weekend, I think, have made it very apparent that even if I had been successful as I hoped I would be in persuading you, Mr. Chief Judge, that this did adequately satisfy the spirit of the Court of Appeals ruling, there would have been those who would have said the president is defying the law.
>
> This president does not defy the law and he has authorized me to say he will comply in full with the orders of this court.

In the days that followed, Nixon also announced that he would appoint a new special prosecutor, as Congress was demanding, and that "we will cooperate with him."

Nixon's gestures of conciliation defused the crisis atmosphere surrounding Watergate, but tensions on this issue were still high. And other problems loomed as well in the fall of 1973.

In foreign affairs, the Soviet Union had been indicating that it planned to send troops to the Middle East, where Israel was fighting its Arab enemies. Because such a move would be a threat to Israel, Nixon put American troops on alert and Moscow backed down.

Another problem was a developing energy shortage caused by decisions made by Arab nations that produce much of the world's oil. In the United States there were higher prices for gasoline, periodic shortages of gasoline, and calls for everyone to turn down their thermostats to save energy.

In the midst of all this, on October 10, 1973, Vice President Spiro Agnew resigned under pressure because investigators had found that he did not pay as much income tax as he really owed. Agnew had never been a very important figure at the White House, but his resignation added to the feeling that everything was falling apart. Nixon chose a well-liked member of Congress, Representative Gerald Ford (Michigan), to replace Agnew.

Nixon was asked at a news conference on October 26 how he was holding up under all these pressures.

Well, those who saw me during the Middle East crisis thought I bore up rather well. I have a quality which is, I guess I must have inherited it from my Midwestern mother and father, which is that the tougher it gets the cooler I get. . . .

There are things which of course do tend to get under the skin of the man who holds this office. But as far as I'm concerned, I have learned to expect it. It has been my lot throughout my political life.

Nixon expanded on this theme two weeks later in a televised speech about the energy shortages.

> I would be less than candid if I were not to admit that this has not been an easy year. As a result of the deplorable Watergate matter, great numbers of Americans have had doubts raised as to the integrity of the president of the United States. I've even noted that some publications have called on me to resign the office of president of the United States. Tonight, I would like to give my answer to those who have suggested that I resign. I have no intention whatever of walking away from the job I was elected to do.

Nixon's determination to stay in office did not reduce the opposition that was building steadily against him. In early November, shortly after the special prosecutor was fired, the *New York Times* and *Time* magazine both urged the president to resign. Other publications followed. Public opinion polls showed that support for Nixon was continuing to erode. A Gallup poll in early November found that three out of four Americans believed that the president was involved in the Watergate scandal.

These doubts—and Nixon's problems—would grow in the months ahead.

13

GAPS GALORE

BECAUSE OF THE PUBLIC OUTRAGE OVER THE FIRING OF AR-
chibald Cox, the White House wasted no time in appointing a
new special prosecutor to continue the Watergate investigations. The man chosen was Leon Jaworski, a sixty-eight-year-
old Texas lawyer who had served on government commissions
before and had been head of the American Bar Association (a
trade group that sets standards for attorneys).

Jaworski was reluctant to take the job after seeing what
had happened to Cox, but the White House assured him that
he would have independence. "It has been discussed with the
president," White House Chief of Staff Alexander M. Haig,
Jr., told Jaworski. "He's willing to let you exercise whatever
independence you need."

Jaworski was still apprehensive, but Haig told the lawyer
it was his duty to take the job. "I'm putting the patriotic
monkey on your back, Mr. Jaworski," Haig said. "The situation in this country is almost revolutionary. Things are about
to come apart. The only hope of stabilizing the situation is for
the president to be able to announce that someone in whom
the country had confidence has agreed to serve." Haig also
promised that Nixon would not fire Jaworski without the consent of congressional leaders. There would be no more Saturday Night Massacres.

Jaworski accepted the job and the appointment was announced in early November. He got to work at once, meeting with the staff Cox had put together.

The first order of business was the White House tapes. Cox had subpoenaed nine of them, as well as a number of presidential papers, and Nixon had finally agreed to turn them over. But more trouble was brewing.

A week after President Nixon agreed to deliver the nine tapes to Judge Sirica, White House lawyers found that two of the tapes did not exist. One of them was a conversation that occurred just three days after the Watergate break-in. It was a phone call on June 20, 1972, between Nixon and John Mitchell, then head of the president's reelection committee.

The second so-called missing tape was of a conversation that took place on the evening of April 15, 1973, between the president and John Dean. During that meeting, Dean had informed the president he was no longer part of the White House team—he was talking to prosecutors about Watergate.

White House attorney J. Fred Buzhardt told Sirica that the president had used a phone not linked to the White House recording system when he spoke to Mitchell on June 20.

Buzhardt said the Nixon-Dean conversation had not been recorded because it had occurred at the end of a busy day of meetings and the tapes were already filled. April 15 was a Sunday and the tapes were not checked on weekends.

Sirica was upset about the missing tapes. First the White House had said that it had them, then it said it did not. Once again, it seemed that the president was failing to deliver.

The judge decided to do what he could to insure that nothing else went wrong. He ordered a hearing and got several people from the White House to testify on what precautions were being taken with the rest of the tapes.

Among those interviewed at the hearing was Rose Mary Woods, Nixon's personal secretary. Woods had been given the job of transcribing the tape recordings—listening to them and writing down what she heard. It was tedious work because the conversations that had been recorded were long and sometimes difficult to hear.

"Were any precautions taken to assure that you did not accidentally hit the 'erase' button?" she was asked.

Woods replied with some disdain, "Everybody said 'be careful,' which I am. I don't want this to sound like bragging, but I don't believe I am so stupid that they had to go over and over it. I was told, 'If you push the button, it will erase,' and I do know, even on a small machine, you can dictate over something [and] that removes it. I think I used every possible precaution not to do that."

Woods was then asked what special precautions she had used to make sure she did not erase anything.

"What precautions?" she said. "I used my head. It's the only one I had to use."

Three weeks later, the White House again shocked the nation. Buzhardt revealed that the first tape Woods had worked on had an eighteen-minute gap in it. The tape, of a meeting between Nixon and Haldeman on June 20, 1972, had included a discussion of Watergate, according to notes Haldeman had taken during the meeting. But, Buzhardt said, the section of the tape dealing with Watergate had been erased, apparently while the tape was being transcribed.

Judge Sirica really was angry this time. He ordered the remaining tapes sought by the special prosecutor delivered to court immediately for safekeeping.

And he brought Woods back for another interview. This time she was not so cocky. Woods said it was she who had accidentally erased part of the June 20 tape while she was transcribing.

She explained that she had been using a large machine that operated with a foot pedal. When she pushed the pedal, the tape moved forward. As she was working on the June 20 tape, she said, the phone behind her rang. She said she tried to push the STOP button on the recorder and leaned back to answer the phone, keeping her foot on the pedal. But instead, she said, she must have hit the RECORD button. Since her foot was still on the pedal, the tape continued running and she erased part of the conversation.

When she got off the telephone and turned back to the

tapes, she immediately realized her mistake. "I must say, after I turned around from the telephone, being someone who has tried to do a good job, I practically panicked," Woods testified. She hurried in to tell the president about the error. Woods said she had been on the phone for five minutes. She could not account for the rest of the eighteen-minute gap.

Because this story sounded so unlikely, Woods's recording machine was brought into court so she could reenact exactly what happened.

Woods dutifully put on the headphones.

"The telephone rings," said assistant Watergate prosecutor Jill Wine Volner. "Would you show us what you did?"

Woods then pushed a button on the machine and leaned back to answer the imaginary phone. But as she leaned, she lifted up her foot, as one normally would in such a position.

That effectively demonstrated the point Volner was trying to make. Anyone stretching back to answer a phone while sitting in a chair naturally would have raised their foot. But the White House stuck to Woods's story. In an attempt to strengthen her case, Woods's lawyer arranged for a photographer to take a picture of her at the recording machine in her White House office, showing how she had kept her foot on the pedal while answering the telephone.

The picture was published in newspapers and magazines all over the world. But instead of bolstering her story, it made poor Rose Mary Woods a laughing stock; hardly anyone believed her. Even those who gave Woods the benefit of the doubt still could not account for the rest of the eighteen-minute gap. If she had been on the phone only five minutes, that left 13 minutes unexplained.

Haig also was asked about the gap and came up empty-handed. But he added that he and the White House lawyers had discussed the possibility that "perhaps some sinister force had come in and . . . taken care of the information on the tape." The idea of a "sinister force" at work in the White House caught the public's imagination. Haig's facetious remark made headlines around the nation.

While Americans were amused by both Haig and Woods,

the eighteen-minute gap further eroded confidence in the president.

Judge Sirica, dissatisfied with the White House's explanations, asked a panel of technical experts to look at the tape and see if they could tell what had occurred. The panel members reported their findings a couple of months later. They concluded that the gap was caused by someone who had erased the tape deliberately, with at least five separate stops and starts.

In all the years since Watergate, no one has ever admitted to erasing the tape. Some people, including Jaworski, suspected that Nixon himself was responsible, but the president denied this in his memoirs. The eighteen-minute gap has remained one of the mysteries of Watergate.

President Nixon's problems mounted steadily during the fall of 1973. He had been in a long-running dispute with the IRS for a tax deduction of $482,000 he had taken in 1970 for donating his private papers to the National Archives. Such deductions for donations of presidential papers—which are valuable to historians—had been allowed in the past, but in 1969 Congress removed this tax benefit for presidents. That meant the deduction Nixon took for his papers was illegal.

The president did finally agree to pay the $482,000 in back taxes; however, he denied having done anything wrong in taking the deduction in the first place. At a meeting of newspaper editors in Orlando, Florida, he said, "I've made mistakes, but in all my years of public life I have never profited from public service. . . . People have got to know whether or not their president is a crook. Well, I'm not a crook. I earned everything I've got."

Many Americans thought it was sad that the president of the United States had to stand up and deny being a crook. At the time, polls showed that three out of four people believed Nixon had lost so much credibility in the Watergate scandal that it was hard for him to be an effective president. Questions about his personal finances just made the situation worse.

It was about this time that Nixon turned over the tapes that had long been sought by the special prosecutor. Judge

Sirica was to listen to them first in private and then pass along to the special prosecutor any segments that might be important to the grand jury's investigation of Watergate.

The judge listened to the tapes in his court chambers with one trusted aide. The atmosphere was such at the time that he had the tape machine checked for "bugs" before he turned it on.

When he finally started to listen, he was shocked. The president, well spoken in public, was vulgar in private. His conversations were full of swear words and ethnic insults. Even worse, Sirica found, the conversations about Watergate were extremely damaging to Nixon.

The judge was especially disheartened by the March 21 tape of a meeting between Nixon and John Dean. At that meeting Dean told Nixon about the Watergate burglars' demands for money, and how one of them, Howard Hunt, was threatening to reveal White House dirty dealings unless he was paid.

To most people this would look like blackmail, pure and simple. But on the tape Nixon expresses no outrage—or even surprise—that someone was trying to blackmail the president of the United States. Instead he told Dean that it would be possible to get $1 million to make payoffs for several years. And he ordered Dean to hurry and get the $120,000 that Hunt was demanding right away. "Would you agree that that's a buy time thing, you better damned well get that done, but fast?" Nixon said to Dean. "Well, for Christ's sake, get it. . . ."

Jaworski had a similar reaction to the blackmail conversation. As a lawyer, listening to the tapes for evidence of criminal wrongdoing, he was depressed by many of the other conversations as well.

To his mind, the first tapes he heard strongly indicated that President Nixon was part of the conspiracy to cover up the Watergate burglary—discussing blackmail payoffs to keep Howard Hunt quiet and coaching his aides to "just be damned sure you say, 'I don't remember, I can't recall,'" when they testified before Watergate investigating committees or grand juries. He heard nothing on the tapes to indicate that the president was shocked by the cover-up or wanted to get the truth out to the American people.

"Listening to him scheme, knowing he was the president of the United States, I felt as if my heart was shriveling inside of me," Jaworski later wrote in his book *The Right and the Power.*

At that point he began gathering evidence that could lead to criminal charges against President Richard Nixon.

14

THE PRESIDENT LOSES KEY SUPPORTERS

AS 1974 BEGAN, PRESIDENT NIXON WAS SEEN IN PUBLIC LESS and less. He celebrated his sixty-first birthday in seclusion at his home in San Clemente, California. When he did make a public appearance he looked tense and tired. Opinion polls showed that Americans were evenly split on the question of whether he should resign.

Despite all of this, said spokesman Gerald Warren, Nixon "is approaching this year in a positive way."

The president himself, in his State of the Union speech to Congress on January 30, 1974, made it clear that he was tired of Watergate and had no plans to step down.

> I have provided to the special prosecutor voluntarily a great deal of material. I believe that I have provided all the material that he needs to conclude his investigation and to proceed to prosecute the guilty and to clear the innocent.
>
> I believe the time has come to bring that investigation and the other investigations of this matter to an end. One year of Watergate is enough.

Nixon said that he would cooperate with the House Judiciary Committee as it investigated whether he had done anything to warrant impeachment. But he added a warning, saying he would not do anything "that weakens the office of the presidency."

Finally, Nixon said, "I want you to know that I have no intention whatever of walking away from the job that the people elected me to do."

Despite Nixon's claim that he had given the special prosecutor all the information he needed, Jaworski was far from satisfied. In a letter to White House attorney James D. St. Clair on February 1, Jaworski noted that he had not received documents he had requested from the White House as far back as November and December. "Will you please advise me whether it is now the position of the president that the office of the special prosecutor is to receive none of the items requested?" he wrote. Without them, Jaworski added, he could not wrap up the grand jury investigations. If "one year of Watergate is enough," he said, he would need quick cooperation from the president.

St. Clair wrote Jaworski a long letter in response, and they had a meeting. But it all amounted to nothing—the White House refused to turn over any more tapes or documents to the special prosecutor.

Jaworski decided to bide his time. He already had enough evidence to bring grand jury indictments against the president's former top aides, although he needed the White House tapes to take the cases to trial. And he felt he also had proof that the president of the United States had cooperated in a criminal conspiracy to cover up the Watergate break-in.

That presented a problem. Jaworski did not think it would be wise to return an indictment against Nixon, even though members of the grand jury were satisfied that there was enough proof to do so.

Because such an action would be without precedent, it was not clear what would happen if a president was formally charged with a crime. Many legal scholars felt that the president was beyond the reach of the courts in a criminal matter because the Constitution clearly outlines another remedy—impeachment by Congress.

Under the U.S. Constitution, the House of Representatives is responsible for deciding whether the president should be impeached (charged with a crime and brought to trial in the Senate). Article 1, section 2 of the Constitution says:

> The House of Representatives shall choose their speaker and other officers; and shall have the sole power of impeachment.

Section 3 of article 1 outlines the Senate's responsibility:

> The Senate shall have the sole power to try all impeachments. When sitting for that purpose, they shall be on oath or affirmation. When the president of the United States is tried, the chief justice shall preside: and no person shall be convicted without the concurrence of two thirds of the members present.

With these constitutional restrictions in mind, Jaworski decided that when the grand jury indicted the president's top aides, Nixon himself would be named as an unindicted co-conspirator. That means that the grand jury thought the president was part of the Watergate cover-up—a "conspiracy" in legal language—but decided not to bring criminal charges against him.

The grand jury that had heard all of the Watergate evidence returned an indictment on March 1 charging seven former top aides to Nixon with conspiring to stop the Watergate investigation and obstructing justice.

Those charged with crimes in the indictment had been among the most powerful men in America a short time earlier: John Mitchell, former attorney general and head of the Committee for the Re-election of the President; H. R. Haldeman, Nixon's chief of staff; John Ehrlichman and Charles Colson, both top Nixon advisers; Kenneth Wells Parkinson, a lawyer for Nixon's reelection committee; Gordon Strachan, a former assistant to Haldeman; and Robert C. Mardian, who had worked for Mitchell at the Justice Department and on the re-election committee.

When the seven men appeared in Judge Sirica's court to hear the charges against them a week later, they were fingerprinted and photographed in mug shots, just like common criminals. It was a humiliating moment for men who so recently had helped set the course of the nation.

President Nixon was not named in the indictment when it was presented in the courtroom. Instead, Jaworski gave Judge Sirica a secret report that included all of the evidence the grand jury had gathered against Nixon. The material was put into a big brown briefcase. It was so full that it became known in the newspapers as "the bulging briefcase."

Jaworski asked Judge Sirica to send this secret material to the House Judiciary Committee, which was considering whether there was enough evidence to impeach the president.

The House Judiciary Committee had been formally authorized to start the investigation on February 4 by the full House of Representatives. The vote was 410 to 4 in favor of the investigation. The House also gave its Judiciary Committee power to issue a subpoena to force the president to turn over whatever material the committee felt it needed.

The chairman of the committee was Representative Peter Wallace Rodino, Jr. (Democrat, New Jersey). He said that the committee would do everything it could to convince the public that "this was the right course."

As soon as the House Judiciary Committee formally began its probe, it obtained permission to look through the files of the Senate Watergate Committee, which had held hearings the previous year.

Rodino also tried to get the evidence that Leon Jaworski had presented to the grand jury. Jaworski refused, saying that it would violate the secrecy that the law requires of grand juries.

But once the grand jury publicly returned indictments against Nixon's top aides on March 1, the need for secrecy was reduced. Jaworski thought it would be all right at that point to give the House Judiciary Committee some of the information he had gathered—information against both Nixon and his aides.

Since the White House did not object, the bulging brief-case was turned over to the House Judiciary Committee. The lawyers who carried it from the courthouse to Capitol Hill had a police guard.

Both the House Judiciary Committee and the special prosecutor wanted more tape recordings from Nixon. Jaworski needed information from the tapes as evidence to use in the trials of the Nixon men who had been charged in the Water-gate cover-up. The committee needed the information to de-cide whether Nixon should be forced from office.

Rodino emphasized that the Constitution gives the House primary responsibility in the impeachment process. "The House is vested with tremendous power here," he said. "It is our inescapable responsibility to do this job, to settle this ques-tion, to assure the American people that we will discharge our duty under the Constitution once and for all."

But throughout the spring of 1974, the White House re-sisted efforts by both Jaworski and Rodino to obtain further information. By April, both men were fed up. First the House Judiciary Committee and then the special prosecutor issued subpoenas requiring the president to produce the additional tapes that had been requested. The committee set an April 25 deadline, while the special prosecutor's deadline was May 2.

On April 29 President Nixon announced his decision. In a speech televised around the nation, he said he would not turn over the tape recordings that had been requested. Instead, he said, he had gotten White House aides to listen to the tapes and write down what they heard. After the irrelevant material had been edited out, he said, the White House had come up with twelve hundred pages of conversations from the tapes, all of it related to Watergate. Those conversations, as released by the White House, became known as the Watergate transcripts.

Nixon said he was sending copies to the House Judiciary Committee as well as making the information public. "I want there to be no question remaining about the fact that the presi-dent has nothing to hide in this matter," he said.

Nixon admitted that the conversations from the tapes

"will embarrass me and those with whom I have talked." But, he said, he believed that the transcripts would show the American people that he had been telling the truth all along. "I know in my own heart that through the long, painful and difficult process revealed in these transcripts, I was trying in that period to discover what was right and to do what was right," said the president. "I hope, and I trust, that, when you have seen the evidence in its entirety, you will see the truth of that statement."

The Watergate transcripts caused a sensation. The Government Printing Office in Washington sold eight hundred copies in three hours on May 1. Paperback books filled with the transcripts were rushed into print and sold millions of copies.

Despite the president's hopes for a favorable reaction, most people were appalled by what the transcripts revealed, even though it was later determined that the conversations most damaging to the president had been edited out. The president had made disparaging remarks about almost everyone. He had sworn so often that the transcripts were dotted with "expletive deleted." He had indicated a desire to get even with everyone who had ever opposed him, and he had used ugly names for Italians, Jews, and other ethnic groups.

The portrait of Nixon that emerged from the transcripts—a hostile, suspicious, vengeful, foul-mouthed man—offended many of his longtime Republican supporters. Representative Robert Michel (Illinois) said he had worked for Nixon's election in the past, but "this is not the kind of man I was recommending." Senator Marlow W. Cook (Kentucky) said that Nixon should resign because of "moral turpitude." Senate GOP leader Hugh Scott (Pennsylvania) described the conversations as "disgusting."

Republican-oriented newspapers that had strongly supported Nixon in the past now called for his resignation or impeachment. The *Chicago Tribune* said, "We have seen the private man and we are appalled." The Hearst papers said that Nixon's conversations on the tapes "amount to an unwitting confession, in which he stands convicted by his own words as a man who deliberately and repeatedly tried to keep the truth from the American people."

Similar sentiments were being expressed by many members of the House of Representatives. On May 9 House minority leader John J. Rhodes (Republican, Arizona) sent a message to the White House via reporters. He said that perhaps Nixon should consider resigning as an alternative to being impeached. Nixon's resignation, Rhodes said, "would probably be beneficial" to Republicans.

Polls showed that the president's popularity was declining rapidly outside Washington as well. The Gallup poll on May 4 said that 42 percent of those who watched Nixon's TV performance came away with a less favorable opinion of him.

With support for the president eroding, word spread that Nixon was likely to resign. The rumors got so intense that the White House felt compelled to respond to them.

On May 10, 1974, White House Press Secretary Ron Ziegler telephoned the *New York Times,* with a statement:

> The city of Washington is full of rumors. All that have been presented to me today are false and the one that heads the list is the one that says President Nixon intends to resign. His attitude is one of determination that he will not be driven out of office by rumor, speculation, excessive charges or hypocrisy. He is up to the battle, he intends to fight it and he feels he has a personal and constitutional responsibility to do so.

The next day, Julie Nixon Eisenhower, the president's daughter, held a press conference. She was accompanied by her husband David (grandson of former president Dwight D. Eisenhower).

Asked if they could foresee any point at which Nixon would resign, David said, "Absolutely not, no."

"He is stronger now than he ever has been in his determination to see this through," said Julie.

A reporter told Julie that he felt he should apologize for

addressing Watergate questions to her instead of to her father and added, "I am not quite sure why you are here to answer these questions."

Julie's response was filled with emotion.

> I am going to try to control myself in answer to the question because it really does wound me. I have seen what my father has gone through and I am so proud of him that I would never be afraid to come out here and talk to any members of the press about resignation or anything else. . . . I am not trying to answer questions for him. I am just trying to pray for enough courage to meet his courage. Really.

The White House received many calls praising Julie's performance. In the final days of the Nixon administration she became the person who spoke out publicly for the family, the one who earned the most sympathy and respect.

But despite the best efforts of Julie and the small band of White House aides who remained loyal to Richard Nixon, no one could turn back the events that were about to engulf the president.

15

SHOWDOWN

PRESIDENT NIXON'S DECISION TO RELEASE TRANSCRIPTS OF some of the White House tapes did not satisfy anyone.

Both the House Judiciary Committee and the special prosecutor continued their efforts to get hold of the actual tape-recorded conversations. They did not trust the transcribed versions put out by the White House, and besides, they wanted tapes of conversations that the president had not chosen to release.

But Nixon was in no mood to cooperate at this stage. He decided that the White House would release no more tapes to anyone. He had done all he was going to do to cooperate in investigations that might force him from office.

White House attorney James St. Clair announced Nixon's decision. The president would simply refuse to comply with the House Judiciary Committee's subpoena, he said. And there was really nothing the House could do about it, short of forcing a showdown between the legislative and executive branches of government, which no one was ready for quite yet.

Nixon also decided to take on Special Prosecutor Leon Jaworski. White House attorney James St. Clair argued in Judge Sirica's courtroom that Jaworski had no legal right to try to force Nixon to hand over the tapes. The president had appointed Jaworski, St. Clair said, and so he had the ultimate power to determine what the special prosecutor did. Jaworski had no right to take the president to court.

Jaworski was furious. This line of argument reminded him of the Saturday Night Massacre, when his predecessor, Archibald Cox, was fired for trying to get the tapes. Jaworski reminded the White House that he had been promised when he took the job that he would have a free hand—including the right to sue in court for the tapes.

The White House assured Jaworski that he was in no danger of being fired, not after the public outcry that occurred when Cox was ousted. Nevertheless, White House attorneys continued to argue that Jaworski had no legal right to force the president's hand in court.

Judge Sirica ruled against Nixon once again. He said that Jaworski had every right to seek the tapes and ruled that Nixon should turn them over to the special prosecutor's office immediately.

St. Clair had anticipated this decision, so he was not upset about it. He announced that he would try to get Sirica's ruling overturned at the next-highest legal level—the U.S. Appeals Court.

Jaworski was happy with the decision but worried about the time it would take to settle the issue if it went through the usual, time-consuming court procedure. The trial of Haldeman, Ehrlichman, and others indicted in the Watergate cover-up was scheduled to begin in September, and it was already the middle of May. The Appeals Court would take weeks to hear arguments and issue a decision. And whatever they decided surely would be appealed to the Supreme Court, which planned to adjourn for the summer in mid-June. That would mean no Supreme Court decision on the tapes until the court started up again in October.

This case was too important to wait so long, Jaworski thought. He decided to ask the Supreme Court if it would hear the case right away, skipping the U.S. Appeals Court altogether.

The Supreme Court seldom agrees to take a case that has not been reviewed earlier by the appeals court, and St. Clair argued that the Watergate case was not important enough to warrant such unusual treatment. He noted that the last time the Supreme Court had allowed lawyers to bypass the appeals court was in the early 1950s, when President Truman took control of the nation's privately owned steel mills during the Korean War. The Watergate case was not of such magnitude, St. Clair said.

But, to the surprise of some legal scholars, the Supreme Court agreed to hear the case of the Watergate tapes right away. It scheduled oral arguments for July 8, 1974. One of the nine justices, William H. Rehnquist, said he would not take part in the case because he had worked earlier at the Justice Department under John Mitchell. He therefore had a conflict of interest.

A large crowd gathered outside the courtroom on the day the lawyers were to argue the case. Many people wanted to witness this historic debate. Some were fervently backing the special prosecutor. "Go Leon," they shouted. Others applauded when St. Clair arrived.

Inside the courtroom, Jaworski spoke first. At the heart of his argument was a challenge to Nixon's belief that he had a constitutional right as the nation's chief executive to withhold the Watergate tapes as an executive privilege. "The president has embraced the Constitution as offering him support for his refusal to supply the subpoenaed tapes," Jaworski said. "Now the president may be right in how he reads the Constitution. But he may also be wrong. And if he is wrong, who is there to tell him so?"

When the point came up again a little later during the court hearing, Justice Potter Stewart responded to the question of Who is there to tell him so? "This court will tell him so," Stewart said. "That is what this case is about, isn't it?"

St. Clair disagreed with Jaworski's assessment. He said that the courts had no right to rule on the question of whether the tapes should be released. That decision was the president's, he argued. It was his executive privilege.

Justice Thurgood Marshall asked, "You are still saying the absolute privilege to decide what shall be released and what shall not be released is vested in one person and nobody can question it?"

"Insofar as it relates to the presidential conversations, that is correct," St. Clair responded.

Two weeks later, on July 24, 1974, the justices issued their decision—an eight-to-zero vote that Nixon must turn over the tape recordings of all sixty-four conversations that had been subpoenaed by the special prosecutor. Jaworski had won the final test on the tapes. Now it was only a matter of time until the tapes themselves would be made public.

On the same day that the Supreme Court ordered Nixon to turn over the tapes, the House Judiciary Committee began public hearings on whether to impeach the president.

Armed with the material Jaworski had provided and other documents, the committee had been meeting in a private session since May 9 to weigh the evidence against the president. It had decided to make the final three days of hearings public, and the proceedings were shown on television across the nation.

Under our Constitution, the House has the right to recommend whether a president should be forced to leave office—to be impeached. The issue is first taken up in the House Judiciary Committee. If it recommends impeachment, the full House votes on the question. If the full House recommends impeachment, the matter then goes to the Senate. The one hundred senators then put the president on trial and make the final decision on his fate. A two-thirds majority vote is required for impeachment in the Senate.

The world watched in fascination as the House Judiciary Committee began its televised hearings. Nothing quite like this had ever happened before; the only other presidential impeachment case occurred right after the Civil War in 1868, when an effort to drive President Andrew Johnson from office failed in the Senate by one vote. Johnson's enemies said he had committed treason by treating the South leniently after the Civil War.

Nixon's case was entirely different. He had been accused of criminal activity.

The Judiciary Committee's public hearings opened July 24 with a motion by Representative Harold Donohue (Democrat, Massachusetts): "I move that the committee report to the House a resolution, together with articles, impeaching the president of the United States, Richard M. Nixon."

The committee had prepared five separate charges against Nixon. Each one was called an article of impeachment and members voted on each charge separately.

Article 1 accused Nixon of obstruction of justice—specifically, of trying to "delay, impede and obstruct" the investigation of the Watergate break-in; of counseling his aides to give false statements to aid the cover-up; of approving payments to buy silence from potential witnesses; and of trying to misuse the CIA.

The committee approved article 1 on a vote of twenty-seven to eleven.

Article 2 charged Nixon with abuse of power. It said that he tried to get the IRS to do tax audits for political purposes; he set up wiretaps for political purposes and misused the FBI and the Secret Service; and he authorized a secret unit in the White House that performed illegal acts, including the break-in at the office of Daniel Ellsberg's psychiatrist in the Pentagon Papers case.

The committee approved article 2 on a vote of twenty-eight to ten.

Article 3 accused the president of defying the House Judiciary Committee's subpoenas for the Watergate tapes.

It was approved too, by a vote of twenty-one to seventeen.

Article 4 focused on Nixon's decision to bomb Cambodia without informing Congress, and article 5 accused the president of income tax fraud.

The committee rejected both of those charges by votes of twenty-six to twelve.

So, during its three days of public hearings, the House Judiciary Committee approved three articles of impeachment against the president. The next step was a vote by the full House.

Republican House members found themselves in a difficult position. Many were disgusted with Nixon but still were reluctant to vote to impeach the leader of their political party.

"I am one that has agonized over this particular inquiry," said Representative Thomas F. Railsback, an Illinois Republican and Judiciary Committee member. But he voted in favor of the first two articles of impeachment, saying, "If we are not going to really try to get to the truth, you're going to see the most frustrated people, the most turned off people, the most disillusioned people. . . ."

Representative Caldwell M. Butler (Republican, Virginia), another Judiciary Committee member, also voted in favor of the first two articles. "If we fail to impeach, we have condoned and left unpunished a course of conduct totally inconsistent with the reasonable expectations of the American people," he said.

While the House Judiciary Committee's hearings were going on, Nixon's aides were saying publicly that they thought the president would win when the full House voted on the impeachment articles. The president, White House Press Secretary Ron Ziegler said, was "confident because he knows he has committed no impeachable offense."

But this confidence was not shared behind the scenes. Republican leaders in the House were counting heads and finding out that the vote against the president would be overwhelming, maybe more than 300 of the 435 House members. Many members of Congress were worried about their own political futures. Voters angry with a Republican president might be inclined to take their disgust out on the local Republican congressman in the November elections.

On August 1 House leaders tentatively decided to start debate on impeachment three weeks later, on August 19. These plans were never carried out, however, because the White House was about to drop another bombshell.

16

THE SMOKING GUN

PRESIDENT NIXON'S LAWYERS BEGAN TURNING OVER TAPES of Watergate conversations to Judge Sirica on July 30, as ordered by the Supreme Court. But a sense of doom had descended upon the White House.

For months the president had refused to allow most of his aides to listen to the tapes. Those that had taken part in the Watergate discussions—Haldeman, Ehrlichman, Dean, Colson—were long gone. The new crew did not know what had been said in the Oval Office during the Watergate cover-up, and Nixon was not eager for them to find out.

In the weeks leading up to the Supreme Court decision, however, Nixon himself had listened to some of the tapes, and after the court ruled, he asked one of his attorneys, J. Fred Buzhardt, to listen to one tape in particular. The recording centered on a conversation between President Nixon and H. R. Haldeman on June 23, 1972, just six days after the break-in at the Watergate. On the tape, the president and Haldeman talked about getting the CIA to slow down the FBI's investigation.

This simple conversation proved devastating to Nixon. He had claimed that he had known nothing about his aides' plans to hide the reelection committee's involvement in the break-in until March 1973, when John Dean explained everything to him.

But the June 1972 tape clearly showed that the president was talking with Haldeman about the cover-up six days after the break-in occurred. So in reality he had known about the cover-up all along, even while he was telling the public that he did not.

The tape also showed that the president had been trying to interfere in the FBI's investigation of Watergate. Nixon claimed that he had sought CIA interference because he was trying to protect America's secrets. But the tape showed that the president had a political motive in calling on the CIA—he did not want the public to know that members of his reelection committee had been involved in the break-in.

Here, from the June 23 tape, is the president telling Haldeman how to convince the CIA to try to curb the FBI investigation of Watergate:

NIXON: When you get these people [the CIA] in, say, "look, the problem is that this will open the whole—the whole Bay of Pigs thing, and the president just feels that," without going into the details . . . don't lie to them to the extent to say there is no involvement, but just say this is sort of a comedy of errors, bizarre, without getting into it—"the president believes that it is going to open the whole Bay of Pigs thing up again."
HALDEMAN: OK.

Later that same day, the tape showed, Nixon again told Haldeman how to convince the CIA to slow down the FBI probe. He repeated the idea of telling the CIA that an FBI investigation would reveal too much about American foreign policy on Cuba, going back to a 1960s operation called the Bay of Pigs.

HALDEMAN: Yeah, that's the basis we'll do it on and just leave it at that.

NIXON: I don't want them to get any ideas we're doing it because our concern is political.
HALDEMAN: Right.
NIXON: And at the same time, I wouldn't tell them it is not political.

The tape-recorded conversation was hard to follow and sometimes confusing. But that last sentence was clear: "At the same time, I wouldn't tell them it is not political."

When Buzhardt listened to this tape, he was convinced that it would drive Nixon from office. But others in the White House were not so sure. They argued that perhaps people would think the president had simply been trying to protect a national secret in asking the CIA to interfere.

Eventually, though, all of the senior aides and lawyers in the White House came around to Buzhardt's way of thinking. They then insisted that Nixon release the tape, because if it was kept secret, the aides could be in trouble too—for covering up important evidence that might be used against the president.

On August 5, President Nixon released the tape-recorded conversation of June 23, 1972. In a speech that was broadcast by television all over America, he admitted that he had misled the public:

> In a formal written statement on May 22 of last year, I said that shortly after the Watergate break-in I became concerned about the possibility that the FBI investigation might lead to the exposure either of unrelated covert activities of the CIA or of sensitive national security matters. . . . I said that I therefore gave instructions that the FBI should be alerted to coordinate with the CIA and to ensure that the investigation not expose these sensitive national security matters.
>
> The statement was based on my recollection at the time—some 11 months later—plus documentary materials and relevant public testimony of those involved.

The June 23 tape clearly shows, however, that at the time I gave those instructions I also discussed the political aspects of the situation, and that I was aware of the advantages this course of action would have with respect to limiting possible public exposure of involvement by persons connected with the re-election committee.

Nixon said he realized that "this additional material I am now furnishing may further damage my case," but added that he hoped Americans would consider all of the evidence, not just the June 23 tape by itself.

Whatever mistakes I made in the handling of Watergate, the basic truth remains that when all the facts were brought to my attention I insisted on a full investigation and prosecution of those guilty. I am firmly convinced that the record, in its entirety, does not justify the extreme step of impeachment and removal of a president. I trust that as the constitutional process goes forward, this perspective will prevail.

But it did not. The June 23 tape was the last straw for many people, both those in Congress who had been supporting Nixon and regular citizens who were reluctant to see any president removed from office.

After Nixon's speech, a quick poll by NBC showed that 62 percent of Americans favored impeachment. And all members of the House Judiciary Committee, even those who had backed the president previously, now said that they would vote for impeachment when the issue came up for a vote by the full House.

"I feel that I have been deceived," said Representative Edward Hutchinson (Michigan), the top Republican on the House Judiciary Committee. He had voted against all of the impeachment charges in committee, believing the president to be innocent.

Representative Charles Wiggins (Republican, California) had been the president's strongest defender during the committee's hearings and also had voted against all of the articles of impeachment. Wiggins was invited to the White House the day before the June 23 tape was released and given a copy so that he would be prepared for what was to follow. After Nixon made the tape public, Wiggins said he had come to the "painful conclusion" that the president should resign. Failing that, Wiggins said, he would vote to impeach the man he had so admired.

By August 7, two days after Nixon released the tape, Republicans estimated that fewer than a dozen of the 435 House members would vote against impeachment. And when the president stood trial in the Senate, they expected at least eighty-five of the one hundred senators to vote to remove the president of the United States from office.

At the White House, Nixon was privately weighing his options. He could go through the constitutional process—an impeachment vote in the House, a trial in the Senate—even though he was sure to lose. Or he could resign and avoid becoming the first president in history to be removed from office by Congress.

On August 7 Nixon met with three top congressional Republicans—Senate GOP leader Hugh Scott (Pennsylvania), Senator Barry Goldwater (Arizona), and Representative John Rhodes (Arizona). "He invited us down this afternoon to disclose to him the actual situation in the House and Senate regarding his position," Goldwater said afterward.

"He asked me [what the outlook was]," Scott said. "I said, 'gloomy.' He said, 'damn gloomy?' I said, 'Yes, sir.'"

That same afternoon, Nixon met with Secretary of State Henry Kissinger. Kissinger returned to the White House that evening and stayed past midnight, talking with the president.

On the morning of August 8 Richard Nixon met with his vice president, Gerald Ford, to tell him what was coming. It was not a long meeting. The two had never been close. In the afternoon Ziegler announced that Nixon would address the nation that night. Word spread quickly throughout the capital and the country.

In the early evening Nixon met with members of his family—his wife Pat, his daughters Julie and Tricia, and their husbands, David Eisenhower and Edward Cox. Julie and Tricia both cried. Julie and her father had a long, sad hug.

Later, Nixon informed the Democratic leaders of Congress of his plans.

Finally, he had a farewell session in the Cabinet Room of the White House with members of Congress who had been his strongest supporters. It was a melancholy meeting; some of the men got teary-eyed.

Shortly before 9:00 P.M. Nixon went to the Oval Office, sat down at his desk, and prepared to speak to the nation. Most Americans, and many foreigners, were watching their TV sets as he spoke:

Good evening.

This is the 37th time I have spoken to you from this office, where so many decisions have been made that shaped the history of this nation. Each time I have done so to discuss with you some matter that I believe affected the national interest.

In all the decisions I have made in my public life, I have always tried to do what was best for the nation. Throughout the long and difficult period of Watergate, I have felt it was my duty to persevere, to make every possible effort to complete the term of office to which you elected me.

In the past few days, however, it has become evident to me that I no longer have a strong enough political base in the Congress to justify continuing the effort. . . .

I have never been a quitter. To leave office before my term is completed is abhorrent to every instinct in my body. But as president, I must put the interest of America first. America needs a full-time president and a full-time Congress, particularly at this time with the problems we face at home and abroad.

To continue to fight through the months ahead for my personal vindication would almost totally absorb the time and attention of both the president and the Congress in a period when our entire focus should be on the great issues of peace abroad and prosperity without inflation at home.

Therefore, I shall resign the presidency effective at noon tomorrow. Vice President Ford will be sworn in as president at that hour in this office.

Ford watched the speech at his home in the suburbs of Washington. Afterward, he went outside to talk with waiting reporters. "I think that this is one of the most difficult and very saddest periods and one of the very saddest incidents that I have ever witnessed," he said.

When Nixon finished speaking, Kissinger walked into the Oval Office and escorted the president out. They parted in the West Wing and Nixon went on alone, to his family. They sat together for awhile. Then the president had a final session with his chief of staff, Alexander Haig.

On his final night in the White House, President Nixon got little sleep. Between midnight and 2:00 A.M. he made more than a dozen phone calls to old political friends and to members of Congress who had supported him. He arose before seven the following morning, August 9, and had a breakfast of grapefruit, milk, and wheat germ.

In the Lincoln Sitting Room he signed his name as president for the final time, in a letter to Henry Kissinger:

Dear Mr. Secretary:
I hereby resign the Office of President of the United States.

At around nine o'clock Nixon said his good-byes to the White House staff. He walked down a line, shaking hands with each of them. Then he gathered up his family and they rode downstairs together on the White House elevator to the East Room, which was filled with members of the cabinet and staff members.

As the Nixon family entered the room, the applause started. It continued for four minutes. Then the president began to speak. He talked about how proud he was of what the administration had accomplished during his five and a half years in the White House.

He talked about his father ("I remember my old man") and described all of the jobs he had had—streetcar motorman, farmer, rancher, grocer. He also talked about his mother. "My mother was a saint," he said.

And he talked about Theodore Roosevelt. He said he had been reading Roosevelt's diaries on his last night in the White House and was struck by a passage Roosevelt had written about his first wife, who died young: "And when my heart's dearest died, the light went from my life forever." Nixon said, "That was T. R. in his 20s. He thought the light had gone from his life forever, but he went on. And he not only became president, but as an ex-president, he served his country always in the arena, tempestuous, strong, sometimes wrong, sometimes right, but he was a man."

Nixon said it was an example that everyone should remember—that when someone loses a loved one, or fails an exam, or loses an election, they think "that all has ended." But instead, the president said, "It is only a beginning always."

By the time he had finished speaking, many in the audience were crying. Nixon and his family left then for the Diplomatic Reception Room on the bottom floor of the White House. Gerald and Betty Ford were waiting for them.

"Good luck, Mr. President," Nixon said.

Outside on the South Lawn, a helicopter was ready. Mrs. Nixon, Tricia, and Ed got on first. Julie remained behind with her husband David. As the president boarded the steps, he turned around and gave her a thumbs up sign. Then he was gone.

Gerald Ford was formally sworn in as president at 12:03 P.M. on August 9 by the chief justice of the Supreme Court, Warren Burger.

"Our long national nightmare is over," Ford said. "Our Constitution works. Our great republic is a government of laws and not of men. Here, the people rule."

EPILOGUE

MOST AMERICANS WERE RELIEVED WHEN RICHARD NIXON resigned, and they welcomed Vice President Ford as his replacement. The tension that had gripped the country for so long abated. An atmosphere of goodwill took its place.

Gerald Ford was popular during his first month in office. A Gallup poll in mid-August showed that 71 percent of the people approved of the way he had taken over, 26 percent were undecided, and only 3 percent disapproved.

Ford chose as vice president a former New York governor, Nelson Rockefeller, and promised to give top priority to the nation's economic problems—inflation and high unemployment.

But the shadow of Watergate was not far away. Even though Richard Nixon had resigned, the possibility loomed that he, as a private citizen, could face criminal charges stemming from the cover-up.

No former president had ever stood trial in federal court before. It was an unsettling thought to many; but polls showed that a majority of the public believed that Nixon, like his aides, should be prosecuted for his wrongdoing.

President Ford did not want to see the nation enmeshed in Watergate again. He decided to ensure that Richard Nixon would not be prosecuted. Article 2, section 2 of the Constitution gives the president "power to grant reprieves and pardons for offenses committed against the United States, except in cases of impeachment." On September 8 Ford announced "a full, free and absolute pardon unto Richard Nixon for all of-fenses against the United States which he, Richard Nixon, has committed or may have committed or taken part in during the period from Jan. 20, 1969, through August 9, 1974" (the five and a half years that Nixon was in office).

The president said that he had been told that it would be many months, and perhaps years, before Richard Nixon could expect to get a fair jury trial in the United States.

> During the long period of delay and potential litigation, ugly passions would again be aroused, our people would again be polarized in their opinions, and the credibility of our free institutions of govern-ment would again be challenged at home and abroad.
>
> My conscience tells me clearly and certainly that I cannot prolong the bad dreams that continue to reopen a chapter that is closed. My conscience tells me that only I, as president, have the constitu-tional power to firmly shut and seal this book.

Nixon accepted the pardon.

> I hope that his compassionate act will contrib-ute to lifting the burden of Watergate from our country. I know many fair-minded people believe that my motivations and actions in the Watergate affair were intentionally self-serving and illegal. I now understand how my own mistakes and misjudg-ments have contributed to that belief and seemed to support it. This burden is the heaviest one of all to bear.

Public reaction to the pardon was swift and unfavorable. Telegrams and letters poured into the White House in protest. Ford's own press secretary resigned in anger. In Congress, Democrats, and some Republicans, were outraged.

Senate Democratic leader Mike Mansfield (Montana) noted that the Constitution says that all men are equal under the law, "and that includes presidents and plumbers." It was not fair to pardon Richard Nixon, he said, when forty or fifty men already had been indicted of Watergate-related offenses and some had gone to prison.

Former Watergate prosecutor Archibald Cox said that in giving Nixon a pardon before he had been charged with a crime, President Ford had undermined several democratic principles, including the one that says "that the law does in truth apply to all men equally."

Senator Hugh Scott supported the president's decision, saying that it would "bring an end to an American tragedy."

Voters, however, were not quite ready to put Watergate aside. They took out their anger in the congressional elections held on November 4, 1974. That year, Democrats gained forty-three seats in the House of Representatives, three seats in the Senate, and four governorships.

Among those who lost their House seats were four Republican members of the Judiciary Committee who had defended Nixon during the nationally televised impeachment hearings. In Vermont a Democrat was elected to the Senate for the first time since the Republican party was founded in 1854. "This is not just a victory, this is a mandate," said Speaker of the House Carl Albert (Democrat, Oklahoma).

The White House was taken aback by the size of the GOP defeat. "It wasn't a very good day for Republicans," press secretary Ron Nessen said in an understatement.

Republicans were not the only victims of Watergate; public enthusiasm for the democratic election process also suffered. Only 38 percent of those eligible to vote turned out on Election Day in 1974, the lowest voting level since 1946. And two years later, Gerald Ford, the Republican nominee for president, was defeated in the general election by a Democrat, former Georgia Governor Jimmy Carter.

But the lessons of Watergate are not all negative. The challenges it posed showed how well our democratic system can operate in a crisis. In many countries, the military simply takes over and ousts the civilian president when trouble occurs. There are no strong traditions or institutions to resolve the problems through other government channels.

In the United States in 1974, the House of Representatives and the Senate were prepared to remove Richard Nixon from office peacefully and install his successor according to the law established in the Constitution. The courts played a crucial role in moving the crisis to that stage.

Nixon's resignation allowed the nation to avoid the pain of seeing a president on trial in the Senate, with the chief justice acting as judge.

But had the president chosen to fight to the end, America's constitutional government would have allowed him to do so. His removal from office was assured either way, in the orderly fashion thought out so carefully by our country's founders.

WHO'S WHO: THE MAJOR CHARACTERS IN WATERGATE

RICHARD MILHOUS NIXON was the thirty-seventh president of the United States, serving from January 1969 to August 1974. He grew up in California, graduated from law school, and served in the navy during World War II. A Republican, he was elected to the U.S. House of Representatives in 1947 and again in 1949, and then served in the Senate from 1951 to 1953. In 1952 he was elected vice president and spent eight years in that job under President Dwight D. Eisenhower. With Spiro T. Agnew as his running mate, he was elected president in 1968. Nixon is the only U.S. president ever to have resigned from office (in 1974). He now lives in New Jersey and frequently writes books on world affairs. In 1978 he wrote his autobiography, *RN: The Memoirs of Richard Nixon.*

H. R. "BOB" HALDEMAN was President Nixon's chief of staff, the most powerful man in the White House next to the president. He wore his hair in a crew cut and had a cold, brusque manner. Nixon once told him, "You're my lord high executioner." Before working on the White House staff, Haldeman worked in advertising. He spent eighteen months in prison for his role in the Watergate scandal. Today he lives in Santa Barbara, California, and is a business consultant.

JOHN D. EHRLICHMAN, a lawyer, was President Nixon's number-two adviser after Haldeman. Ehrlichman and Haldeman met when they were in college at the University of California at Los Angeles. During the 1960s Haldeman recruited Ehrlichman to work for the Nixon campaign. Like Haldeman, Ehrlichman served eighteen months in prison for his role in the Watergate cover-up. Today he lives in Santa Fe, New Mexico.

JOHN DEAN was counselor to President Nixon, meaning that he was the White House lawyer. But he was a minor figure among the Nixon men and was little known in Washington before Watergate. His decision to tell the nation the true story of the cover-up in the summer of 1973 made him a national star. He served four months in prison on a charge of conspiring to cover up the Watergate break-in and later wrote a best-selling book about the ordeal, *Blind Ambition.*

JOHN N. MITCHELL was President Nixon's friend and law partner before Nixon became president. He served as Nixon's campaign manager in 1968. Mitchell was attorney general during Nixon's first term in office but resigned to become chairman of the president's reelection committee in 1972. He served nineteen months in prison for his role in Watergate. Mitchell, who lived in Washington, died in 1988 at age seventy-five.

CHARLES W. COLSON, a top aide to President Nixon, devised some of the most devious plans put forth while Nixon was president. But during the seven months he spent in prison on obstruction of justice charges, Colson became religious. Today he runs Prison Fellowship Ministries in Washington.

JEB STUART MAGRUDER, the number-two man on President Nixon's reelection committee, sat in on the meetings that led to the break-in at the Watergate. Magruder served seven months in prison. He became a minister when he got out, and he now lives in Columbus, Ohio.

G. GORDON LIDDY was a one-time FBI agent who, upon John Dean's recommendation, was sent to work with the president's reelection committee. Liddy put together the plan that led to the Watergate break-in. After the burglars were caught he told John Dean that he was willing to be shot if it would help.

E. HOWARD HUNT, JR., was a spy for the CIA for twenty-one years before he began doing undercover work for the Nixon White House. He was in the Watergate helping to direct the burglars the night they were caught.

JAMES W. McCORD, JR., like Hunt, worked for the CIA for more than twenty years. In January 1972 he was hired as security coordinator for the president's reelection committee, and he still held that job when he was arrested during the burglary at the Watergate.

BERNARD L. BARKER, FRANK A. STURGIS, VIRGILIO R. GONZALEZ, AND EUGENIO R. MARTINEZ were the other four Watergate burglars. All four lived in Miami and were brought into the Watergate operation by Hunt, who had worked with them during his days in the CIA.

JOHN J. SIRICA, chief judge of the U.S. District Court in Washington, D.C. presided over the trials of the Watergate burglars and, later, the White House officials involved in the Watergate cover-up.

ARCHIBALD COX was the first Watergate special prosecutor, an outsider hired because the Justice Department had failed to get to the bottom of the story. President Nixon fired him in October 1973 in what became known as the Saturday Night Massacre.

LEON JAWORSKI was the second Watergate special prosecutor. He and President Nixon fought a battle in the Supreme Court over tape recordings that Nixon had made of his conversations. Jaworski won.

SAM ERVIN, a Democratic senator from North Carolina, was chairman of the Senate Watergate Committee.

BOB WOODWARD AND CARL BERNSTEIN were reporters for the *Washington Post* who discovered much of the secret information about Watergate before other reporters did. They won a Pulitzer Prize for their work, and a movie, *All the President's Men,* was made about them.

L. PATRICK GRAY, JR., was a lawyer who became friends with Richard Nixon and subsequently got a number of government jobs. Nixon nominated him to be director of the FBI in May 1972 but withdrew the nomination the next year after Gray admitted to burning papers related to the Watergate case.

CHRONOLOGY

1972

June 17. Police arrest five burglars found in the offices of Democratic National Chairman Larry O'Brien at the Watergate hotel-apartment-office complex in Washington, D.C.

June 18. President Nixon puts a top aide, John Ehrlichman, in charge of finding out about the break-in.

June 19. James McCord, one of the Watergate burglars, is fired from his job as security coordinator of President Nixon's reelection committee.

The Justice Department announces that it has started an investigation of the Watergate break-in.

June 22. At an informal news conference, the president denies any White House involvement in the break-in.

June 25. Martha Mitchell, wife of John Mitchell, the president's campaign manager, telephones reporter Helen Thomas. Mrs. Mitchell says she will leave her husband because of "all those dirty things that go on" in the presidential campaign.

June 28. G. Gordon Liddy, who planned the Watergate break-in, is fired from his job with Nixon's reelection committee.

July 1. John Mitchell resigns from the Nixon reelection committee so that he may tend to "the happiness and welfare of my wife and daughter."

August 1. The *Washington Post* reveals that a $25,000 check contributed to President Nixon's reelection campaign had been deposited into the bank account of one of the Watergate burglars.

August 23. President Nixon is nominated for a second term in office at the Republican National Convention. The vote is 1,347 to 1.

August 29. President Nixon says at a news conference that White House lawyer John Dean conducted a thorough investigation into the Watergate matter and that "his investigation indicates that no one in this administration, presently employed, was involved in this very bizarre incident."

September 15. A federal grand jury indicts the five Watergate burglars, along with G. Gordon Liddy and E. Howard Hunt, who helped coordinate the break-in. They are accused of bugging telephones and stealing papers from the Democratic National Committee.

September 17. Liddy, Hunt, and the five Watergate burglars all plead not guilty and are released from jail on bond.

November 7. President Nixon wins reelection in a landslide against the Democratic candidates, Senator George McGovern.

1973

January 8. The trial of the Watergate burglars begins in the courtroom of District Court Judge John J. Sirica.

January 10. Howard Hunt, one of the defendants in the Watergate trial, pleads guilty to charges of conspiracy, burglary, and wiretapping.

January 15. Four of the Watergate burglars, following Hunt's lead, plead guilty. They deny that they were forced to enter the guilty plea.

January 20. President Nixon is inaugurated for a second term in the White House.

January 30. The jury in the Watergate trial finds G. Gordon Liddy and James McCord guilty. They were the only two charged who did not plead guilty to the charges.

February 2. Judge Sirica says he is not satisfied that the full story of Watergate came out during the trial.

February 7. The Senate votes to set up a special committee to investigate Watergate.

February 28. The Senate begins hearings to decide if it will approve L. Patrick Gray to be director of the FBI. Gray tells the senators that when the FBI was investigating the Watergate break-in, it showed its secret reports to John Dean, the president's lawyer.

March 10. Charles Colson, the White House aide who gave directions to Howard Hunt, resigns.

March 21. John Dean tells President Nixon that "a cancer is growing on the presidency" because of Watergate.

March 23. Judge Sirica reads a letter from Watergate burglar James McCord that says that not everyone involved in the Watergate burglary has been identified. McCord also says that some witnesses lied during the burglars' trial.

March 26. The federal grand jury that indicted the Watergate burglars meets again to hear new charges related to Watergate.

March 28. In a secret session of the Senate Watergate Committee, James McCord testifies that John Mitchell, John Dean, Charles Colson, and Jeb Magruder (a top aide to Mitchell) knew about the Watergate break-in before it occurred.

March 30. John Dean hires a criminal lawyer.

April 2. Dean's lawyer tells the government prosecutors who are presenting evidence to the Watergate grand jury that Dean will talk freely.

April 5. The White House withdraws its nomination of Gray as FBI director.

April 14. Jeb Magruder tells the Watergate prosecutors that he is involved in the Watergate cover-up. He also names others who are involved.

April 30. President Nixon announces the resignations of John Dean, John Ehrlichman, H. R. Haldeman, and Attorney General Richard Kleindienst. The president replaces Kleindienst with Elliot Richardson and adds that Richardson will have the power to appoint a special prosecutor to investigate Watergate.

May 17. The Senate Watergate hearings open.

May 18. Harvard lawyer Archibald Cox is appointed special prosecutor to investigate Watergate.

June 6. Nixon announces that Alexander Haig will replace H. R. Haldeman as the White House chief of staff.

July 16. White House aide Alexander Butterfield reveals that President Nixon has tape-recorded all of his White House conversations since 1970.

Senator Sam Ervin, head of the Senate Watergate Committee, sends Nixon a letter asking to see any tapes that contain Watergate-related conversations.

July 18. Archibald Cox, also seeking the tapes, writes the president.

The president's taping system is disconnected.

July 23. President Nixon refuses to turn over any tapes to either Ervin or Cox. Cox and the Senate committee both issue subpoenas for the tapes.

August 29. Judge Sirica orders President Nixon to give him the tapes that Cox subpoenaed on July 23. Sirica says that he will listen to the tapes and decide whether the Watergate grand jury should hear them.

August 30. The White House announces that it will appeal Judge Sirica's ruling to a higher court.

October 10. Vice President Spiro Agnew resigns after deciding not to fight a charge that he failed to pay part of his income taxes.

October 12. President Nixon nominates Gerald Ford as vice president.

October 20. The White House announces that President Nixon has abolished the special prosecutor's office and ordered that Archibald Cox be fired because he continued to demand the tapes. Attorney General Richardson resigns rather than fire Cox; his deputy, William Ruckelshaus, is fired for refusing to fire Cox. The number-three man at the Justice Department, Robert Bork, fires Cox and is named acting attorney general.

October 23. The White House announces that President Nixon will obey Sirica's order and turn over the tapes he requested.

October 23–24. In the House of Representatives, forty-four Watergate-related bills are introduced; twenty-two call for impeachment of the president or for the House to look into the idea, twelve call for a new special prosecutor. Eight impeachment resolutions are sent to the House Judiciary Committee.

November 1. Leon Jaworski, a lawyer from Houston, is named as the new special prosecutor.

November 21. The White House reveals in court that there is an eighteen-minute, fifteen-second gap on a tape-recorded conversation between President Nixon and H. R. Haldeman on June 20, 1972, three days after the Watergate break-in.

December 21. Jaworski receives the subpoenaed White House tapes from Judge Sirica.

1974

February 14. Jaworski says the White House has refused to give him additional tape recordings and papers he needs for his investigation.

March 1. The federal grand jury hearing Watergate evidence indicts seven former presidential aides, including Haldeman, Ehrlichman, and Colson, who had the most powerful jobs in the

White House in 1973. They are charged with lying to the FBI and the grand jury and making payoffs to the Watergate burglars to keep them from talking.

April 30. Under pressure from the House Judiciary Committee and Jaworski, the White House copies down conversations from the president's tape recordings and releases these transcripts publicly.

May 1. The House Judiciary Committee tells the president that the transcripts are not enough; it wants to hear the tapes themselves.

May 7. A White House lawyer says that President Nixon will not turn over any further tapes to either Jaworski or the House Judiciary Committee.

May 9. The House Judiciary Committee begins hearing evidence that will help it decide whether to impeach the president. The hearings are closed to the public.

May 24. Jaworski appeals to the Supreme Court in an effort to get White House tapes of sixty-four conversations related to Watergate.

July 8. The Supreme Court hears arguments from Jaworski and the White House on whether the president should be forced to turn over tapes of the sixty-four Watergate conversations that Jaworski is seeking.

July 24. The Supreme Court rules unanimously that President Nixon must turn over the tapes requested by Jaworski. The White House says that Nixon will comply with the order.

July 27. The House Judiciary Committee approves an article of impeachment accusing the president of obstructing justice in the Watergate case.

July 29. The House Judiciary Committee approves a second article of impeachment accusing Nixon of abuse of power.

July 30. The House Judiciary Committee approves a third article of impeachment accusing the president of defying subpoenas for the Watergate tapes.

The president turns over tapes of eleven of the sixty-four subpoenaed conversations to Judge Sirica.

August 2. The president turns over thirteen more taped conversations.

August 5. President Nixon makes public transcripts of three conversations he had with H. R. Haldeman on June 23, 1972. The transcripts show that Nixon tried to get the CIA to stop the FBI from investigating Watergate.

Support for the president collapses after he reveals the June 23 tape.

August 8. In a televised speech to the nation, President Nixon announces: "I shall resign the presidency effective at noon tomorrow."

August 9. Gerald Ford is sworn in as president of the United States.

SUGGESTED READINGS

BOOKS BY WATERGATE FIGURES

Dean, John. *Blind Ambition*. New York: Simon and Schuster, 1976.

Ehrlichman, John. *Witness to Power*. New York: Simon and Schuster, 1982.

Haldeman, H. R., and Joseph DiMona. *The Ends of Power*. New York: Quadrangle, 1978.

Liddy, G. Gordon. *Will: The Autobiography of G. Gordon Liddy*. New York: St. Martin's Press, 1980.

Magruder, Jeb Stuart. *An American Life*. New York: Atheneum, 1974.

McCord, James W., Jr. *A Piece of Tape. The Watergate Story: Fact and Fiction*. Rockville, Md.: Washington Media Services, 1974.

BOOKS BY WATERGATE INVESTIGATORS

Ben-Veniste, Richard. *Stonewall*. New York: Simon and Schuster, 1977.

Dash, Samuel. *Chief Counsel—Inside the Ervin Committee—the Untold Story of Watergate*. New York: Random House, 1976.

Ervin, Sam, Jr. *The Whole Truth: The Watergate Conspiracy*. New York: Random House, 1980.

Jaworski, Leon. *The Right and the Power*. New York: Readers Digest Press, 1976.

Sirica, John J. *To Set the Record Straight*. New York: W. W. Norton, 1979.

Thompson, Fred D. *At that Point in Time*. New York: Quadrangle, 1975.

BOOKS BY REPORTERS

Bernstein, Carl, and Bob Woodward. *All the President's Men*. New York: Simon and Schuster, 1974.

Lucas, Anthony. *Nightmare: The Underside of the Nixon Years*. New York: Viking, 1976.

Mankiewicz, Frank. *U.S. vs. Richard M. Nixon: The Final Crisis*. New York: Quadrangle, 1975.

Sussman, Barry. *The Great Cover-Up: Nixon and the Scandal of Watergate*. New York: Thomas Y. Crowell, 1974.

White, Theodore H. *Breach of Faith*. New York: Atheneum, 1975.

Woodward, Bob, and Carl Bernstein. *The Final Days*. New York: Simon and Schuster, 1976.

REFERENCE BOOKS

Karnow, Stanley. *Vietnam: A History*. New York: Viking Press, 1983.

New York Times. *The End of a Presidency*. New York: Bantam Books, 1974.

New York Times, ed. *The Watergate Hearings. Break-in and Cover-up*. New York: Viking Press, 1973.

Presidency 1974. Washington, D.C.: Congressional Quarterly, 1974.

Washington Post. *The Presidential Transcripts*. New York: Dell, 1974.

Watergate and the White House, vols. 1–3. New York: Facts on File, 1973–74.

Watergate: Chronology of a Crisis, vols. 1 and 2. Washington, D.C.: Congressional Quarterly, 1973–74.

INDEX